ARCH

BY

DESIGN

ARCHAEOLOGIST'S TOOLKIT

SERIES EDITORS: LARRY J. ZIMMERMAN AND WILLIAM GREEN

The Archaeologist's Toolkit is an integrated set of seven volumes designed to teach novice archaeologists and students the basics of doing archaeological fieldwork, analysis, and presentation. Students are led through the process of designing a study, doing survey work, excavating, properly working with artifacts and biological remains, curating their materials, and presenting findings to various audiences. The volumes—written by experienced field archaeologists—are full of practical advice, tips, case studies, and illustrations to help the reader. All of this is done with careful attention to promoting a conservation ethic and an understanding of the legal and practical environment of contemporary American cultural resource laws and regulations. The Toolkit is an essential resource for anyone working in the field and ideal for training archaeology students in classrooms and field schools.

ARCHAEOLOGY BY DESIGN

STEPHEN L. BLACK
KEVIN JOLLY

ARCHAEOLOGIST'S TOOLKIT
VOLUME 1

ALTAMIRA
PRESS

A Division of Rowman & Littlefield Publishers, Inc.
Walnut Creek • Lanham • New York • Oxford

AltaMira Press
A Division of Rowman & Littlefield Publishers, Inc.
1630 North Main Street, #367
Walnut Creek, CA 94596
www.altamirapress.com

Rowman & Littlefield Publishers, Inc.
4501 Forbes Boulevard, Suite 200
Lanham, MD 20706

PO Box 317
Oxford
OX2 9RU, UK

British Library Cataloguing in Publication Information Available

Library of Congress Cataloging-in-Publication Data

Black, Stephen L.
  Archaeology by design / Stephen L. Black and Kevin Jolly.
      p. cm. — (Archaeologist's toolkit ; v. 1)
Includes bibliographical references and index.
  ISBN 0-7591-0397-6 (alk. paper) — ISBN 0-7591-0020-9 (pbk. : alk.
paper)
  1. Archaeology—Research. 2. Archaeology—Methodology. I. Jolly,
Kevin. II. Title. III. Series

CC83 .B58 2002
930.1'028—dc21
                                          2002014277

Printed in the United States of America

♾™ The paper used in this publication meets the minimum requirements of
American National Standard for Information Sciences—Permanence of Paper
for Printed Library Materials, ANSI/NISO Z39.48-1992.

 CONTENTS

SERIES EDITORS' FOREWORD

The Archaeologist's Toolkit is a series of books on how to plan, design, carry out, and use the results of archaeological research. The series contains seven books written by acknowledged experts in their fields. Each book is a self-contained treatment of an important element of modern archaeology. Therefore, each book can stand alone as a reference work for archaeologists in public agencies, private firms, and museums, as well as a textbook and guidebook for classrooms and field settings. The books function even better as a set, because they are integrated through cross-references and complementary subject matter.

Archaeology is a rapidly growing field, one that is no longer the exclusive province of academia. Today, archaeology is a part of daily life in both the public and private sectors. Thousands of archaeologists apply their knowledge and skills every day to understand the human past. Recent explosive growth in archaeology has heightened the need for clear and succinct guidance on professional practice. Therefore, this series supplies ready reference to the latest information on methods and techniques—the tools of the trade that serve as handy guides for longtime practitioners and essential resources for archaeologists in training.

Archaeologists help solve modern problems: They find, assess, recover, preserve, and interpret the evidence of the human past in light of public interest and in the face of multiple land use and development interests. Most of North American archaeology is devoted to cultural resource management (CRM), so the Archaeologist's Toolkit focuses on practical approaches to solving real problems in CRM and public archaeology. The books contain numerous case studies from all parts of the continent, illustrating the range and diversity of applications. The series emphasizes the importance of such realistic considerations as budgeting, scheduling, and team coordination. In addition, accountability to the public as well as to the profession is a common theme throughout the series.

Volume 1, *Archaeology by Design*, stresses the importance of research design in all phases and at all scales of archaeology. It shows how and why you should develop, apply, and refine research designs. Whether you are surveying quarter-acre cell tower sites or excavating stratified villages with millions of artifacts, your work will be more productive, efficient, and useful if you pay close and continuous attention to your research design.

Volume 2, *Archaeological Survey*, recognizes that most fieldwork in North America is devoted to survey: finding and evaluating archaeological resources. It covers prefield and field strategies to help you maximize the effectiveness and efficiency of archaeological survey. It shows how to choose appropriate strategies and methods ranging from landowner negotiations, surface reconnaissance, and shovel testing to geophysical survey, aerial photography, and report writing.

Volume 3, *Excavation*, covers the fundamentals of dirt archaeology in diverse settings, while emphasizing the importance of ethics during the controlled recovery—and destruction—of the archaeological record. This book shows how to select and apply excavation methods appropriate to specific needs and circumstances and how to maximize useful results while minimizing loss of data.

Volume 4, *Artifacts*, provides students as well as experienced archaeologists with useful guidance on preparing and analyzing artifacts. Both prehistoric and historic-era artifacts are covered in detail. The discussion and case studies range from processing and cataloging through classification, data manipulation, and specialized analyses of a wide range of artifact forms.

Volume 5, *Archaeobiology*, covers the analysis and interpretation of biological remains from archaeological sites. The book shows how to recover, sample, analyze, and interpret the plant and animal remains most frequently excavated from archaeological sites in North America. Case studies from CRM and other archaeological research illustrate strategies for effective and meaningful use of biological data.

Volume 6, *Curating Archaeological Collections*, addresses a crucial but often ignored aspect of archaeology: proper care of the specimens and records generated in the field and the lab. This book covers strategies for effective short- and long-term collections management. Case studies illustrate the do's and don'ts that you need to know in order to make the best use of existing collections and to make your own work useful for others.

Volume 7, *Presenting the Past*, covers another area that has not received sufficient attention: communication of archaeology to a variety of audiences. Different tools are needed to present archaeology to other archaeologists, to sponsoring agencies, and to the interested public. This book shows how to choose the approaches and methods to take when presenting technical and nontechnical information through various means to various audiences.

Each of these books and the series as a whole are designed to be equally useful to practicing archaeologists and to archaeology students. Practicing archaeologists in CRM firms, agencies, academia, and museums will find the books useful as reference tools and as brush-up guides on current concerns and approaches. Instructors and students in field schools, lab classes, and short courses of various types will find the series valuable because of each book's practical orientation to problem solving.

As the series editors, we have enjoyed bringing these books together and working with the authors. We thank all of the authors—Steve Black, Dave Carmichael, Terry Childs, Jim Collins, Charlie Ewen, Kevin Jolly, Robert Lafferty, Brian Molyneaux, Kris Sobolik, and Lynne Sullivan—for their hard work and patience. We also offer sincere thanks to Mitch Allen of AltaMira Press and a special acknowledgment to Brian Fagan.

LARRY J. ZIMMERMAN
WILLIAM GREEN

1

DESIGNING ARCHAEOLOGICAL RESEARCH WITH AN ATTITUDE

Archaeology is expensive, time-consuming, and, as Kent Flannery put it, "the most fun you can have with your clothes on." Envisioning and articulating a research strategy is a creative exercise that forces you to consider carefully all the contexts of an archaeological project: the players, the laws, the physical environment, the cultural setting, the logistical constraints, and the state of our shared archaeological knowledge. A well-designed research project allows you to target, acquire, and analyze the data needed to address meaningful, interesting research problems while coping with the often competing interests of sponsors, regulators, peers, and the public. The task of designing your research is one of the most essential, intellectually stimulating, and engaging aspects of archaeology. And you can do it with your clothes on.

This volume explains the process of designing archaeological research. It begins with an overview of the archaeological research process, emphasizing the value of carefully built research design in all projects. The book then identifies the conceptual tools needed to do archaeology effectively, and it focuses on ways to plan for and implement successful projects.

While the focus here is on research mandated by federal and state laws, or cultural resource management (CRM) archaeology, much of the approach we advocate applies equally to academic and grant-funded archaeological research. The steps presented here aren't the last word in designing archaeological research, but they reflect the best of what we've seen work and the worst of what we've seen fail. What we've noticed more than anything else is the importance of attitude. The key difference between good, interesting research and boring, worthless projects can be traced right back to attitude.

Every time we archaeologists go to the field, we are given an opportunity to learn something new about past humans and their landscapes. And to gain those hard-won insights, we often destroy or make way for the destruction of the very remains, deposits, and patterns that provide those insights. We need to take the attitude that each research opportunity is precious, that our shared archaeological heritage is built of thousands of small things, that every time we attack the archaeological landscape, the archaeological record will gain more than the landscape has lost. We just need to make the most of each and every research opportunity.

The way that we do that is by stating our assumptions, our plans, and our intentions before we hit the field. We lay out our approach to a particular project or research question and then explain what we're going to do, how we're going to do it, and what we think we will find. Designing archaeological research allows our peers, sponsors, and regulators to become engaged in our research, rather than to simply be consumers of the bare facts and arcane interpretations we generate at the final bell. More important, though, when we design our research, we engage ourselves. We give ourselves the ability to make the most of the research opportunity, for our own satisfaction and for posterity as part of the ever-growing archaeological record.

It's that attitude—making the most of opportunity—that is archaeology by design.

THE PROCESS OF DESIGNING ARCHAEOLOGICAL RESEARCH

Designing archaeological research is a process. The first product generated from that process is the research design. Research designs don't all look alike. Sometimes a research design may be part of your response to a request for proposals (RFP), or it could be part of a permit application, grant proposal, internal memo, or even a term paper. Like any other tool, what it looks like isn't important. Marshalltown and Goldblatt trowels both do the job equally well in skilled hands. What is important is that the cutting edge is sharp, the handle strong, and, most critically, that it is guided by a keen observer. Research designs can take many different forms and can be written (or remain unwritten) for quite different audiences. But to accomplish effective archaeological research, your research design should entail five critical things:

The Five Essential Elements of a Research Design

- A research context
- Explicit research questions
- Definitions of the data you plan to collect
- A plan to present your work and results
- Accommodation to the real world

Your research design should reflect a larger set of goals—a research context for your work. In CRM archaeology, many projects will seem so small that you might think they don't need a research design. But multiply those small projects by a hundred or a thousand a year, and you're looking at a sizable chunk of archaeology. That's why you always need to identify a research context for your work. It might be a favored theoretical framework, a regional research design developed by your state historic preservation officer (SHPO), a personal research agenda, or an institutional research focus. Whatever it is, likely a combination of several of these, this larger research context is what allows you to fit your specific research design (and your work) into the larger body of archaeological knowledge and contribute to the field. No matter what kind of project it is, large or small, your research design can help ensure that your work contributes to our understanding of the archaeological record.

Your research design should spell out a set of explicit research questions. These can be framed as questions, problems, or hypotheses—different forms of the same thing—a device for giving your research direction. The focus of your questions can be broad or narrow but should match the scope of the project. While a ten-mile pipeline survey is not likely to produce data bearing on the origins of plant domestication, it might help evaluate a regional model of Early Archaic site distribution (or, more likely, produce the data needed to convince a utility company to consider an alternative route). By making your research questions explicit and appropriately focused, you can create a research environment where your planned data collection methods and analytical strategies are firmly and rationally linked to larger goals (scientific goals, management goals, regulatory goals, preservation goals, etc.). The kicker here (and the fun) is to create research questions that are interesting and meaningful within a larger research context.

Your research design should define the data that will be collected to address the research questions. Tied inexorably to the data itself are the methods used to collect it. This portion of the design is really a methodological overview and a guide to how you hope the work will be done. Once in the field, as all experienced archaeologists know, reality takes precedence. Changes in soil conditions, access arrangements, weather, unexpected deposits, and equipment problems all conspire to thwart the most finely laid plans. It may sound backward, but this is where explicit plans are the most critical. If you've carefully defined your methods and the data you hope to collect, then when changes need to occur, your research design will serve as a guide for making systematic changes in the methods (and data), so that the research focus of your project remains intact.

Your research design should provide an after-the-field plan for analyzing and reporting your work. An often overlooked component of an effective research design is that it should spell out an intended analytical approach. The worst time to begin thinking about how you're going to analyze the materials from an archaeological project is when the fieldwork is complete. Once you've hit the lab, there is too much to do and never enough time to do it. And if there is no plan in place, you'll likely fall back on standard descriptive "analyses" that produce reams of paper but precious little data that actually speak to an identified research problem. By defining the analytical approach up front (and modifying it as the fieldwork progresses), you can leave the field ready to begin the analytical chores at hand. An added plus is that by planning for analysis and focusing analyses in purposeful directions, you can often free up time on the back end to explore the new and different questions that inevitably arise through the course of your work and to pursue innovative ways of presenting the work.

Finally, your research design should accommodate the real world. Your research doesn't exist in a scientific vacuum. It happens or fails to happen in a swirling world of business, politics, media, government, personal interaction, tight schedules, juggled budgets, and capriciously enforced bureaucratic policies. The CRM arena is everyday life itself, a world changing so fast that most of us feel like we can't keep up. A preoccupation with the human past may be a soothing antidote to the modern world, but you can't sustain your research unless you pay keen attention to the real world. And reality impacts even the archaeologists who enjoy the sheltered academic world. Like it or not, the real world is a critical part of a successful research design.

With the attitude that every project is a research opportunity, these five core elements build a solid base for an effective research design. But don't lose sight of the real end product of the process of designing archaeological research and the ultimate reason you create a research design in the first place: the research.

PROFESSIONAL ARCHAEOLOGICAL RESEARCH

The real world of archaeological research for most of us employed as archaeologists in North America today lies in the burgeoning field of cultural resource management (CRM). CRM archaeologists in both the public and private sectors spend over half a billion dollars a year complying with and enforcing the various federal, state, and local laws in place to protect and manage archaeological resources. Academic-based and grant-funded archaeology comprise a much smaller piece of the research pie, both in the number of practitioners involved and in the pool of funding available. CRM archaeology and academic research are two different worlds, and the disparities in funding, in research strategies (or the lack thereof), and in perceived status have led to well-developed animosities between practitioners in the two worlds. The animosities can be very real, and they stem from very real differences in the research worlds within which the two groups operate. To design effective research in either world, you must understand the research world in which you operate and work within its peculiar constraints.

ACADEMIC RESEARCH

In the academy, designing research is often initiated in one of three ways. In archaeology-as-science, things get started when the professorial protagonist (and her graduate students) pose some scientifically scintillating research problem tied to an often dense theoretical discourse. They submit a formal research design to the National Science Foundation and, if funded, sally forth (often in some Third World country) to test their ideas in a rigorous fashion. In archaeology-as-culture-history, the research begins with a promising place, a region, or a time period about which not much is known. The professorial protagonist (and his graduate students) may prepare a formal research design and seek government funding or, more likely, develop a short problem statement and a flier for a university field school. Either way, he takes his graduate student assistants and undergraduate student workforce into the field (usually not too far from home), secure in the assertion that their hard work will surely fill in worthwhile gaps in the ever-accumulating record of archaeological knowledge. In classical archaeology, and in the methodologically similar archaeology often done in the centers of high civilization in the New World, things first unfold when the professorial protagonists (and their graduate students) set out on a foreign expedition to uncover some unexplored tell, ancient metropolis, or unplundered tomb. Here the strategy is discovery on a grand scale, though the work may be couched in scientific terms. A prospectus is prepared, grants are sought from the National Geographic Society, and donations are solicited from wealthy philanthropists. Funding in hand, they head out (usually to some Third World country) year after year to dig big holes and find something spectacular enough to fund the next season.

In academic research, you (or the big cheese who heads the project) have the opportunity to choose where to work and what problems to work on. You may need permission or permits from national, state, or local governments, and your chances for tenure, another permit, or another grant may depend on your publication record, but you rarely have a legally binding obligation to publish your results or even to finish your research project (although you do have an ethical obligation!). As a professional archaeologist with graduate school in your rear-view mirror, you will be able to take academic approaches to archaeological research only if you manage to land a tenure-track teaching job or have independent means.

CULTURAL RESOURCE MANAGEMENT RESEARCH

In the CRM world, research design starts in government offices, business suites, corporate headquarters, and law offices with a decision that will impact or destroy archaeological deposits. Usually the driving force is progress—new highways, buildings, drainage improvements, pipelines, and a hundred other reasons to move dirt and lay steel and concrete. These agency heads, CEOs, lawyers, and politicians rarely care or think about the human past: they want the future, and they want it now. Archaeology is not even an afterthought until someone down the bureaucratic food chain realizes that their project won't move forward, and their large budgets will languish unspent until those pesky archaeological sites have been dealt with. Then the archaeology happens. In a hurry.

The research design starts with the area of potential effect (APE), drawn by an engineer or an architect whose interest is the compressibility of the soil, not the depth of the A horizon or the boundaries of an ancient campsite. Depending on the size of the construction budget—and in proportion the size of the budget for archaeological research—a government archaeologist may get involved to focus the work more finely. An advertisement in the *Commerce Business Daily* may announce the project, and if you're interested, you request a copy of the RFP. This document can call for anything from a general bid to "survey four hundred acres for cultural resources" to a massively detailed data mitigation plan (such as a large-scale excavation to salvage archaeological information in advance of an impending construction project). To get the money to do the work and win the opportunity to learn more about the archaeological record of the APE, you must successfully meet the requirements of the RFP. No ifs and no buts, not much wiggle room, and no extra points for a brilliant theoretical framework. That's the way it is in the CRM research world.

Assuming you meet the RFP's technical specification, you must also figure out how to do the work for less than what your competitors charge. Once you've successfully won a project, there are binding contracts with nonperformance clauses, line-item budgets, and deliverables. If all this sounds frighteningly restrictive, keep in mind that as a CRM archaeologist, you will be dealing with budgets and resources that most academic archaeologists can only dream about. For most budding professional archaeologists today, these things will form the reality of your research world, and they will profoundly shape and color the way that you design your research.

A VERY SHORT HISTORY OF CRM ARCHAEOLOGY

Beginning with the Depression-era federal make-work programs in the 1930s and continuing after World War II with the Smithsonian River Basin surveys, large-scale government-funded archaeological research was done and managed by academic archaeologists and their best students. This was the era of "salvage" archaeology, rescuing or salvaging what could be learned and collected before government-funded reservoir projects flooded many of the nation's rivers. The money was modest, and the archaeology of the day was basic culture history—big digs at big sites. Most of the money was spent on fieldwork, resulting in massive and minimally studied artifact collections and comparatively few published accounts. There was little competition among the universities because the money was doled out to the relatively few established programs in parts of the country where reservoirs were being built. There was a close working relationship between the academic archaeologists interested in North America and the small number of government archaeologists at the Smithsonian and the National Park Service.

As the salvage era drew to a close in the 1960s, the consensus approach of culture history came under attack by young academic hotheads like Lewis Binford. For the next decade or more, the ivory tower swayed in turmoil as the "New Archaeology" blossomed on the scene. Amid lots of incomprehensible rhetoric, "archaeology with a capital S," as Flannery put it—Science—took hold. With the manifesto that archaeologists needed to follow an explicitly scientific approach and seek to learn about cultural processes instead of culture history, the need for purposeful research design came to the fore. It wasn't enough to seek out interesting places to dig, expose architecture, amass artifacts, and establish sequences. The archaeological record was far more complex and difficult to understand than had previously been acknowledged. Dead cultures could not be reconstructed, even on paper. Understanding cultural processes and the complicated patterns of human evolution required a new paradigm— a different model of how archaeology should operate. And academic archaeologists began to explore, argue about, and champion all sorts of scientific and pseudoscientific investigative pathways.

While this theoretical and methodological fray was taking place, "contract" archaeology was born with the passage of the Reservoir Salvage Act of 1960, the National Historic Preservation Act (NHPA) of 1966, and the National Environmental Protection Act of 1969. The NHPA was particularly influential because it said that when the federal government is involved in any way in land development and land use, cultural resources must be taken into consideration. Implementing regulations and amendments to this act and the passage of other federal and state laws extended and institutionalized the new field of cultural resource management (see sidebar 1.1). Over the next several decades, funding for archaeology grew by leaps and bounds. Government money coupled with overall economic and population growth also led to the establishment of departments of anthropology and the creation of new contract programs at many smaller state universities and colleges. Few of the university-based contracting programs were integrated with the academic departments. Most were stand-alone (or weakly linked) programs that depended solely on contracts for continued existence.

In the late 1960s and early 1970s, the university-based contract programs did almost all of the research projects that the swelling

1.1. WHAT THE HECK IS A CULTURAL RESOURCE?

Cultural resources can be all kinds of things, but the ones that matter in CRM are the ones that are recognized by the National Register of Historic Places (NRHP) and spelled out in section 106 of the National Historic Preservation Act (NHPA). For these purposes, cultural resources are things and places. The cultural resources that section 106 seeks to preserve are the physical manifestations of cultural activities—stuff that can be managed and preserved. Archaeology is only a part, and actually the smaller part, of the national historic preservation effort. A much larger part of what are considered cultural resources under state and federal laws consists of the built environment. (See King 1998 for a comprehensive treatment of cultural resource laws and practice.)

The National Register places cultural resources into five classifications: buildings, structures, objects, sites, and districts. *Buildings* are buildings—houses, barns, and train stations, for example. If there's only part of a building or only a foundation, it's usually considered a ruin and is classified as a site, not a building. Most historic archaeological sites are classified as sites rather than buildings. *Structures* are things like bridges, dams, and grain elevators—basically anything built that can't be classified as a building. *Objects* are things that are built but that are smaller than structures or are decorative in nature, such as boundary markers, monuments, or fountains. *Sites* are places on the landscape that are either associated with some significant event or person or contain information important to history or prehistory. Sites can be natural features such as a spring or a hill as well as cultural features such as a battlefield, a place where important ceremonies took place, or an archaeological site. *Districts* are areas with a concentration of buildings, structures, objects, or sites that are thematically linked in some way. The individual features in a district don't have to be particularly significant in and of themselves because a district is viewed as more than the sum of its parts.

Section 106 of the NHPA deals with all of these cultural resources. While archaeologists are concerned mostly with archaeological sites, a whole raft of managers, historians, architects, and even cultural anthropologists work with other pieces of the cultural resource pie. Historians and architects focus primarily on documentation and on preserving and sometimes restoring cultural resources as they appeared during the time that they were historically significant. In contrast, archaeologists are often interested in preserving the *information* represented by the patterns of materials at a site. In many parts of the CRM world, practitioners have developed interests or expertise in several areas and may wear several cultural resource hats.

ranks of government archaeologists couldn't do themselves. As more programs sprang up, academic contractors began competing head-to-head with one another for projects. But many academic-trained archaeologists, both those in government who were issuing the contracts and those who were contractors, proved to be poor administrators and poor judges of the real costs of doing solid research. There was little quality control, few established rules, and not much accountability. For a while it didn't matter because the pace was so fast—always a new contract to spend from while the old one was being finished. This vicious spiral eventually caught up with many programs, and university officials began pulling the plug. By the mid-1970s, it was obvious that the universities couldn't meet the increasing demand for work, and private contracting firms were springing up all across the country.

By the mid-1970s, CRM archaeology had already developed a bad reputation from the harried work pace, cutthroat bidding, atheoretical approaches, excessive government regulation, and shoddy reporting. It is equally important to recognize that it wasn't all thorns—lots of good archaeology was being done in the contract world of the day. Some contract programs were well administered and effectively exploited the many opportunities to do meaningful archaeological research. Excellent scientific research designs were drawn up and executed. Many young professional archaeologists learned firsthand how to read the dirt—they investigated more archaeological sites in a decade than most academic archaeologists did in a lifetime. They also wrote some fine reports and, to a lesser extent, scholarly articles that presented solid data and keen insight into the archaeological record. Dedicated government archaeologists fought within their agencies to put genuine concern for cultural resources in the mainstream of decision making. A conservation ethic—the idea that sites should be protected for the future whenever feasible—was widely embraced. The seeds of both the worst and best of today's CRM archaeology were firmly planted.

By the mid-1980s, much of the archaeological work across the country was being done by private consulting firms. These for-profit businesses ranged from one-person firms to large environmental and engineering consulting firms in which archaeology was just one of the services offered. The growth of private consulting firms was paralleled by increasing numbers of federal government archaeologists in the big, land-holding agencies (like the Forest Service and the Bureau of Land Management [BLM]), big land development agencies (the U.S.

Army Corps of Engineers), and many smaller agencies. It wasn't just the federal government that hired archaeologists; state governments and even some local ones did, too. Government archaeologists did regulatory work, they did archaeological contracting, they did public service, and some of them even did research. Archaeology had irrevocably escaped the academic world.

WHY CRM ARCHAEOLOGY HAS A BAD REPUTATION

It's the truth. Academic archaeologists have looked askance at CRM or "contract" archaeology for years. Even within the ranks of CRM archaeology, there is a certain pervasive and perverse self-loathing that diminishes and minimizes the work of thousands of professional archaeologists as not quite "real" archaeology. But this bad reputation is only partly deserved, and it is completely within the power of the current archaeological generation to refute.

A primary reason for its bad reputation is that CRM archaeology generally happens in a hurry. Slice it how you will, haste really does make waste when it comes to learning about the human past. Academic archaeologists take their sweet time because they have to: Good research ideas take time to develop and a heck of a lot of concerted effort to investigate. In the academic world, scholarship really does matter, and it is consistently rewarded. It's a lot harder to come up with thought-provoking questions and carefully honed scholarly publications when progress means looking over your shoulder and considering a lower bid. The speed with which CRM archaeology proceeds has led to the worst aspect of CRM: archaeology by default. Too much archaeological research that is rushed to the field, through the lab, and out the door is ill-considered, boilerplate technical garbage that adds little or nothing to the archaeological record.

If you want to design and carry out effective archaeological research in the world of CRM archaeology, you'd better know what you are getting into. CRM archaeology is young, and many of the problems and pitfalls can be traced to its youth. Its history is still unfolding, its future uncertain. It also has incredible potential to do interesting and effective archaeological research—but only if you learn the system and position yourself to take advantage of the opportunities that will come your way.

Most professional archaeologists today and in the foreseeable future will make their living in the world of CRM archaeology. Whether you're a regulator, an agency archaeologist, or a private contractor, your world will revolve around compliance-driven research. As the twenty-first century begins, the world of CRM archaeology is continuing to mature and become institutionalized. The formation of a trade association, the American Cultural Resources Association (ACRA) in 1995, and the 1998 establishment of the Register of Professional Archaeologists (ROPA) are signs that the field may be coming together to deal with the problems and potentials in modern CRM archaeology. You have a chance to help by being part of that maturing process.

But you can't just trot out your academic training, puff out your chest, and claim the high road of science. You have to be pragmatic and smart and figure out how to balance science with government and business. It is not an easy path to follow; in fact, there really isn't much of a path at all. It's up to us practicing professional archaeologists, CRM and academic alike, to change CRM's bad reputation. The good news is that the surest way to do this is to make our work more interesting, more challenging, more useful, and more fun, by designing our research with an attitude.

WHY DESIGN ARCHAEOLOGICAL RESEARCH?

Designing archaeological research—creating a concrete plan—is where every research project should start and end. If it's done well, it focuses your thoughts and energies so you can make the most of your time and resources. It provides a context for making difficult field decisions. It directs the analysis into areas that are (or should be) interesting and productive. It provides a structure for reporting your work and results. A good research design can help keep archaeological research interesting, productive, and fun. More than that, though, as a researcher involved in the destruction of the archaeological record, as a steward of (mostly) public money, and as a member of a professional community, you have extra obligations that should color the attitude you bring to the work.

Modern archaeology is expensive, and you are responsible for delivering value for the money that you will spend. For CRM archaeologists, the American public supports the preservation laws that provide the opportunity to explore the archaeological record, and you owe them much more than a slap and a tickle when it comes to presenting your research. When methods are unconsidered, data are collected by default—and the archaeology, the analysis, and the conclusions are short-changed. Finally, if designing research is approached as a hurdle, a technical hoop, a box to be checked, then the whole point of doing archaeology is missed. It's thinking, and planning, and analyzing, and understanding that is archaeology—real archaeology that does a service to the archaeological record, the public, and the discipline.

THE COST OF ARCHAEOLOGY

Modern archaeology costs a lot because it is labor-intensive. The federal government alone spends more than a quarter-billion dollars each year on CRM archaeology, and state and private sponsors may spend twice that or more. Most CRM labor is provided by workers with college degrees. Lots of them have acquired highly specialized knowledge in graduate school and through years of on-the-job training. While archaeologists are not paid very well by the standards of many other professions, most of us with graduate degrees and experience get paid $30,000 to $60,000 per year. Archaeology often requires a large labor force. The work is usually far enough from home so that you have to pay to house and feed these folks. Even if the average "field technician" gets paid poorly, when you start multiplying the number of weeks times the number of crew members and then add in the salaried supervisors, travel, housing, food, equipment, and supplies, we're talking serious money.

After the fieldwork ends, the analysis begins. It can be labor-intensive as well, particularly for excavation projects. The longer you dig, the more you haul back to the lab for processing and analysis. In the heyday of culture history archaeology, the analytical emphasis was on describing, classifying, and illustrating the artifacts, usually only the complete tools and whole vessels. This trend carried over into CRM archaeology. Over time archaeologists started looking at and analyzing (or attempting to) all the artifacts they recovered—whole, broken, tools, flakes, sherds, everything. There is, however, only so much you can learn from artifacts alone. Simply processing those collections takes time and money. Since the 1960s, archaeologists have spent more and more time studying bones, plant remains, soils, rocks, snails, residues, and a dozen other types of evidence. Radiocarbon dating has become routine and often costs over $500 for a single sample. A lot has been learned, but many of these materials require specialized study and hard-science analytical techniques. Like everything, analytical and curation costs have gone up and up.

Modern archaeology takes lots of skilled people, lots of specialized analyses, and lots of time—and money. But the expenditure of big piles of money does not guarantee that the research will be worthwhile. In fact, a substantial portion of the money being spent on archaeology today is misdirected to pro forma archaeology done by technicians who rely on default ways of doing things because the boss didn't invest the time to develop a thoughtful research strategy.

YOUR OBLIGATION TO THE PUBLIC

As a CRM archaeologist, you have a weighty obligation to the public. They are the ones whose interest and support for the human past and historic preservation caused the laws to be passed that brought CRM archaeology into existence. They are also the ones who pay for almost all CRM archaeology. In a very real way, your future as a professional archaeologist depends mightily on the continued support of the American public. If we archaeologists screw up our opportunities much longer, there is a very real chance that the laws and regulations will be weakened as the public loses its interest and faith in what we do.

Sounds heavy, doesn't it? It is, and, as a group, CRM archaeologists are just starting to own up to our obligation to the American public. It's finally dawning on us that the golden goose is starting to get pissed.

First, we have to consistently strive to spend our research dollars wisely. This means we have to think carefully about the work we propose and make sure that the research we accomplish is worthwhile. We have to cultivate the attitude that we should get the most we can from each opportunity—to provide value for the money, to justify the faith the public puts in us as archaeologists, and to help understand and preserve the past. When the public sees a project wasting money, they are quick and ruthless. At the same time, most folks are very reasonable if there is a good reason for the money to be spent, a plan in place, and evidence that the project is moving in a positive direction. You're spending the public's money, and unless you'd like to join the $600 hammer and the $1,000 toilet seat in the annals of government waste, you must have a well-conceived plan for performing your research.

Second, we have to give back to the public a much greater share of what we are learning. Our dull technical prose won't cut it. Neither will our endless preoccupation with hair splitting. The public wants to see the big picture and enough of the details to make it interesting, understandable, and believable. In plain English. On the TV. On the Web. In popular books. We have to make our research relevant and interesting to the American public. Not all of it, especially not all the split hairs and abstract discussions, but enough of it so people will know why understanding and preserving the human past is important. If you want your project to succeed in the increasingly public arena of CRM archaeology, and if you want the public to continue to support our profession, you'd better have a plan for sharing some of what you learn with the interested public. It's part of your research design.

ARCHAEOLOGY BY DEFAULT

Many decisions in archaeology are made simply out of habit, following established traditions for reasons that may or may not make sense today. It's worth remembering that CRM archaeology is, to a significant degree, a continuation of the culture history approach to archaeology. So is academic archaeology. Many of the field traditions that characterize American archaeology today, academic and CRM alike, were originally developed to address the chronological and artifact-oriented questions that characterized American archaeology in the mid–twentieth century.

The classic example is excavation by uniform and arbitrary metric units like the one-meter square and the ten-centimeter unit level. Such rote digging became widespread in this country to permit minimally skilled field workers to maintain basic provenience while digging deep or big holes. It replaced the wholesale strip mining for artifacts and unsystematic digging that characterized archaeology in the early twentieth century and represented an important improvement. It persists today in this country to an extent unknown in virtually all other areas of the world. We personally have dug hundreds of square holes, sometimes to good effect, sometimes not, but almost always out of habit, convenience, and tradition.

The square hole method works pretty well when you are digging test pits in unknown territory to answer basic exploratory questions. It sometimes works well in block excavations, particularly those

where the stratigraphy is uncomplicated. But all experienced archaeologists realize that arbitrary units don't work very well when the
stratigraphy is complex and subtle. The standard units invariably result in the mixing of things from different strata that should be kept
separate. European archaeologists have developed much more sophisticated, if sometimes difficult-to-execute, systems of stratigraphic excavation and recording. Yet the one-meter square is still the first thing
that most beginning archaeologists in this country learn to recognize
as the basic excavation unit. Square hole archaeology is a tradition and
a very widespread default method in American archaeology. The implications of the method—constrained data sets, limited spatial resolution, and arbitrary artifact associations—are seldom mentioned in
either research design or analysis.

While the square hole and many other field traditions are common
to both academic and CRM archaeology, default methods are particularly rampant in all aspects of CRM work: field, lab, and reporting.
Unthinking acceptance of the status quo often results in rote, mechanical work in which the participants are merely going through the
motions of the process rather than concentrating on making and con-
veying the critical observations.

The fast-paced, competitive world of CRM archaeology provides
many reasons to have standard methods. If we had to reinvent the
one-meter square or a laboratory data entry form on every project, we
wouldn't get very much dirt moved or data processed. In each archaeological region there are standard approaches to typical problems. For instance, archaeologists in the arid West often rely on
surface survey and collection to locate and begin to evaluate sites,
while those in the wooded East often use shovel tests for these purposes because sites there are buried or shrouded in dense vegetation.
It's not the approach, standard or innovative, that matters but how
you apply that approach to the particular circumstances for the research you're doing.

Standard methods should be explicitly justified just like anything
else: by weighing the costs against the benefits. If there are compelling reasons for using them, fine. But if there is a potentially better, less costly, more informative way to learn what we need to and
intelligently sample the archaeological universe in front of us, then
let's try it. When we approach problems by falling back on the intellectually lazy use of archaeology by default, we shortchange the archaeology and ourselves.

DESIGNING RESEARCH IS ARCHAEOLOGY

Archaeology is more than digging holes, counting potsherds, classifying arrowheads, and obtaining radiocarbon dates. We have to recognize the complexity of the human past in light of the fact that most of it is unknowable. The archaeological record is static, dead as a doornail, and decaying and being destroyed continually. We can, however, learn real verifiable, replicable things about the static archaeological record. Using a scientific approach, we can formulate and test ideas for explaining the cultural processes and causal links that account for the patterns we find in archaeological deposits. But there are also widely accepted ways of doing archaeological research that aren't based in science. Archaeology survives and even thrives as a hobby, culture history, a technical service, and a business. These models work fine if that's all archaeology is meant to be. But for the true professional archaeologist, the fun, the excitement, the joy of archaeology is in learning new things and discovering patterns we didn't know existed—coming to human terms with tiny bits of an almost unknowable past. We design archaeological research to develop a strategy for learning those new things.

The attitude you bring to designing your research should acknowledge these things and use them to focus your work. The design you create is just a tool. If you need to clean a profile for a photograph, the first thing you'll likely do is grab a file and sharpen the edge of your trowel. A research design is like that file: You use it to hone your ideas, your methods, your strategy, so when you bear down on that face (or site), you're not gouging valuable (and costly) hunks from the archaeological record. A research design is a tool you use to organize and present your ideas, lay out your plan of attack, and connect the results that will be produced by your chosen field techniques to the problems you want to address.

2

BUILDING YOUR
PROFESSIONAL TOOLKIT

To design effective research—research that will contribute to our knowledge of the archaeological record, research that allows you to reach achievable goals, and research that will be engaging, fun, and interesting—you need more than attitude: you need tools. You need tools that provide a good grounding in archaeology in general and the regional archaeology where you plan to work in specific. You need tools to understand the range of multidisciplinary options available for examining and analyzing archaeological deposits. You needs the tools to place your work in the context of the regional and fieldwide understanding (or misunderstanding, as the case may be) of the archaeological record. You need tools to manage the bureaucratic and political environment in which your research lives and dies. And you need the tools to manage the day-to-day tactical and long-term strategic business planning that ensures the crew is paid and the truck has gas.

Before anything starts, you need to have your tools sharp and ready to work, and designing archaeological research is no exception. Good, interesting, effective archaeological research flows directly from the time you spend investing in these tools. It's all too easy to spot a project that's been done by folks who view archaeology as little more than hunting for arrowheads and slapping together a table of artifacts and a sketchy site map. To design and execute effective research and make a contribution to the field, you have to first load and then lug your professional toolkit. Here's a quick overview of the tools you'll need.

ANTHROPOLOGICAL ARCHAEOLOGY

The very first thing to load into your toolkit is a good, up-to-date understanding of the goals, history, theory, and methods of modern archaeology and its mother discipline, anthropology. While many archaeologists trained in the Old World see archaeology as part of history and classics, most American archaeologists are trained in anthropology. Archaeologists with a solid foundation in anthropology are more capable of understanding and explaining the material things we dig up than are those who have only technical training in archaeology.

Included in this anthropological foundation should be a basic overview of physical anthropology. Humans represent just one peculiar branch of millions of years of primate evolution, and we share many behaviors and physical characteristics with our fellow apes (members of the superfamily Hominoidea). We need to understand behaviors as controlled by biology and have a good grasp of how the human body responds to challenges like disease, pregnancy, poor nutrition, and extreme climates. Knowledge of primate behavior and human physiology will help you ask interesting questions about the human past. You will also gain insights into why leading experts—like male silverbacks defending their territory—often act like such thuggish jerks.

By studying sociocultural anthropology you learn that biology doesn't explain it all. Humans are social critters who develop and pass along complex behaviors that override and go beyond our genetically conditioned habits. Culture is learned and socially transmitted human behavior. You need a good working knowledge of how human societies, large and small, work—how people are organized or not, how they make a living, how they interact with others, how their belief systems are (or are not) related to the material things that will become the archaeological record.

Along with a good introduction to sociocultural and biological anthropology, you will need to know more about the many aspects of the subdiscipline of archaeology. An appreciation of the history of archaeology is essential because it gives you a strong sense of how young the discipline is relative to most fields of inquiry and because you'll learn how rapidly archaeology has changed over the past century. A strong grounding in field methods is obviously essential. We are endlessly amazed (depressed, really) at how many so-called archaeologists can barely wield a trowel, recognize a soil change, or use a transit. But technical skills are all too mechanical if you are clue-less about theory. Sure, too much of what passes for theory in ar-chaeology is abstract word juggling and half-baked borrowing from the hard sciences, but you really do need a theoretical perspective—an explanatory framework within which you will operate—and you need to know how to articulate that perspective.

Beyond method and theory is analysis—the process of assembling and assimilating the field data and figuring out how to wring useful information from the sherds, bones, and stones that we dig up. All ar-chaeologists should have at least a basic introduction to the gamut of analytical techniques that may prove essential.

A solid high school education followed by a four-year college degree in anthropology should give you most of what you will need to get started and get your archaeological feet wet. Once you have some real field experience and an inkling of what it will take to stay gainfully employed in archaeology, you will realize that most career paths in-volve graduate training. Increasingly, the more responsible and better paying positions in archaeology are held by those with at least a mas-ter's degree. In one sense, an advanced degree is just a piece of paper, a jumped hoop. But more importantly, graduate school is a chance to learn the things you didn't learn in college. To make it really count, you need to know what you want to learn before you get there so you can figure out how to structure your experience to your advantage.

CURRENT ARCHAEOLOGICAL METHOD AND THEORY

Method and theory are often trotted out like a cute pair of twins that get "oohed" and "ahhed" over but then get wheeled back into the house when the real work starts. To do effective and interesting re-search, your methods must be explicit, well defined, and replicable. You employ your methods within a research context defined by one or many theoretical perspectives. Theory is much more than the ab-stract ideas jawed over in a graduate seminar: It is the foundation for productive archaeological research. Your theoretical approach helps you define the data you expect to recover and how you will utilize the data in your analysis. Your methods determine the data you do re-cover. This is worth saying again: Your methods determine your data. You must have an explicit and clear understanding of the implica-tions of the methods you choose on the data you hope to collect. All effective work starts with a solid foundation in method and theory.

Things change, constantly. The way we look at sites, the way we analyze archaeological deposits, and the questions we ask change through time. They all change because we've got new people, new theories, and new methods coming down the pike every day. You don't want to chase every fad that gets pumped into the mix, but you do want your research to be fresh and interesting. The only way to avoid stale, overworked (boring) approaches and to steer clear of the current "pet rock" approach is to maintain an active interest in the field as a whole. It's important, although often difficult, to maintain intellectual energy when doing CRM work. One way you can keep the mental buzz going is by paying attention to new ways of doing things. Are there new dating techniques that might apply to questions you'd like to ask about your site? Are there new ways of collecting and analyzing archaeological information that you might make use of? New ideas and ways of doing things feed the process of creating new, interesting, and exciting research.

MULTIDISCIPLINARY STUDIES

Even an archaeological generalist should have an appreciation for and a basic understanding of other archaeologically related disciplines: biology, botany, paleontology, geology, geography, mathematics, chemistry, and physics as well as history, literature, art, and sociology. Don't squawk yet—you don't need to dedicate your life to these things, but you should be familiar with them and how they impact the work you do in archaeology. For instance, archaeometric dating techniques often come from methods pioneered in paleontology, high-energy physics, or even lunar exploration. You'll be a more effective designer of archaeological research if you have an appreciation for the many different fields that archaeology can involve. Learn to take advantage of opportunities to learn from and work with folks in other related fields.

Enough? Heck no. Newcomers are often surprised to learn that much of the daily life of an archaeologist revolves around things that seem to have absolutely nothing to do with archaeology. Things like managing a budget, hiring and firing people, and running an effective meeting are generally taught in business school. Things like writing and producing an interesting report mean training in writing and a basic understanding of the mechanics of publishing. Archaeologists need many skills beyond the ones that you will get with a degree in anthropology. A smart and far-thinking archaeologist-in-the-making (or one trying to catch up) needs to focus on the whole pie rather than just a single slice. Most of us can't do everything and shouldn't try. But all of us can benefit from understanding how all the pieces and parts fit together.

If you're unfamiliar with managing a budget or hiring people, pick up one of the thousands of how-to books on the market, and give yourself a quick course. The business details of managing an archaeological project are just as critical as the research plan. If you botch a project because of poor management, the damage to the archaeology is just as real as if you'd bulldozed the site. When you can manage your resources effectively, you'll produce more and better work and make a greater, more positive impact on the body of archaeological knowledge.

KEEPING CURRENT

Keeping your knowledge current is just as important as a having a good background. New ideas, theories, and methods appear on the scene almost daily. It's important to keep up with these changes, because staying engaged in the discipline—talking, writing, and e-mailing with folks about real archaeology—keeps you energized and makes archaeology more stimulating. Keeping current simply means staying engaged in the field—engaged with archaeology—with the people and the literature. You should join national, state, and local archaeological societies and participate as actively as you can (see appendix A, "Groups You Should Join"). Meetings are where you meet colleagues, hear what others are learning about, check out the newest books, and otherwise "network" (Latin for rubbing elbows while drinking beer and stretching the truth). One of the best professional favors you can do for yourself is to give professional and popular talks to archaeological groups and community groups. It is the best way to focus your ideas, hone your communication skills, and engage yourself—and others—with what fascinates you about archaeology.

The journals and newsletters that archaeological societies produce are your first line of reference (see appendix B, "Journals You Should Read"). There is no better place to stay current on the thinking, research contexts, and new insights in a region than the local and regional society journals. The importance of keeping up with the literature can't be overemphasized. If an archaeologist loses touch with the field, it is all too common that his work becomes stale, his reports and papers become stale, and he himself becomes stale and bored—"There's just nothing new out there." Just a few hours a month skimming the journals and reading a few articles of interest can keep your interest and imagination piqued.

DEVELOPING REGIONAL EXPERTISE

To do truly effective research, you will need to develop an intimate familiarity with the region where you work—the landscape, its history, its environment, and its material culture. Regional experts make their name because they are interested in and knowledgeable about the total package of things that influence the archaeological record: environment, climate, geology, history, and politics. This kind of wide-ranging appreciation for a region takes sustained interest and a long-term investment. We have seen more than one archaeologist who has a deservedly top-notch reputation in their research region but who has an equally well-deserved reputation for sloth and incompetence outside that region. Understanding your research region is a critical tool in your professional toolkit.

First and foremost, you need to have a clear understanding of the physical landscape and the dynamic natural and cultural processes that form and define the landscape. While the principles that govern such forces are pretty much uniform worldwide (remember Sir Charles Lyell), the landscape of any region on Earth has distinctive characteristics and patterns that you will need to understand (see sidebar 2.1). That way you won't waste time sinking fifty-centimeter-deep shovel tests across terraces where the archaeological deposits are likely buried by ten meters of Holocene sediment.

Natural landscapes are more than just rocks, soils, and streams. Archaeologists also need to develop an appreciation for the unique regional mix of plants and animals that form the ecological systems in which past peoples lived (see sidebar 2.2). You need to adopt an ecological perspective if you are to make much progress in understanding the archaeology of your region, particularly when dealing with prehistoric remains. This means you need to learn about how climatic changes have affected the landscape and the distribution of its plants and animals.

You also need a firm grasp of the culture history of the region. Who were the peoples who lived and settled in your region (see sidebar

2.1. GEOARCHAEOLOGY

Geoarchaeology is the application of geological science to archaeology. Archaeologists in some parts of the world have long worked closely with geologists. Today, many archaeologists are being trained in both fields. This is a natural development because few geologists are trained in and truly interested in the relatively short-lived phenomena and recent time frames that archaeologists typically deal with. Well-trained geoarchaeologists understand archaeological questions and situations and are able to apply appropriate geological methods. Today, geoarchaeologists have their own scholarly journal (*Geoarchaeology*) and hold academic positions in anthropology and geological science departments as well as private and government CRM jobs. Geoarchaeologists are often integral members of archaeological research teams. Their knowledge of the physical landscape often provides crucial contextual information for archaeologists.

The growth of geoarchaeology has caused archaeologists to become more aware of the depositional circumstances in which archaeological deposits are found and more knowledgeable about how such deposits are transformed by erosion, soil formation, and other processes. For instance, it is now being recognized that many of the artifact-rich sites and deposits once simplistically regarded as "occupations" are *palimpsests*—accumulations from many occupations that formed on stable land surfaces and that are often blended in the active biological zones known as soils. Such contexts can yield important information but only when studied for what they are. Through geoarchaeological work, we are now learning how to find and target context-rich, though often artifact-poor, deposits that have greater potential to address many behavioral and ecological questions.

2.3}? What is the current perception of the sequence and timing of events and basic patterns in the archaeological record? What are the important gaps in knowledge? These are the historical contexts within which your analysis and conclusions must operate.

Last, but certainly not least, you need a good handle on the material culture of the region. Not every archaeologist needs to be a Zen master at pottery typology, but you must be able to recognize and evaluate the artifacts, features, and other materials you'll be encountering. You need this knowledge so you can grasp the significance of what you find in the field and use that information to make informed decisions.

The place to start becoming a regional expert is with the current regional experts and what they write. Their reports contain references

2.2. ECOLOGY AND ARCHAEOLOGY

Ecology is the study of organisms and their environmental relationships. Ecological approaches to archaeology and anthropology, often termed *human* or *cultural ecology*, are robust scientific frameworks. Ecological approaches are particularly useful when archaeologists deal with the vast stretch of preindustrial human existence. Hunter-gatherers and other technologically "primitive" peoples had a complex relationship with the natural world, much more complex and interesting than the simple, romantic notion of the "noble savage." Cultural-ecological studies around the world show that this idyllic view of ancient people at one with nature is a modern fantasy. Past societies often failed or were drastically altered by their own ecologically unsound practices. Similarly, natural disasters such as volcanic eruptions and prolonged droughts have profoundly altered human history, recent and ancient.

For the archaeologist, an ecological approach is often attractive because, unlike most ancient cultural systems, many natural ecosystems have survived, albeit in ever-smaller patches. Ecological studies of plants and animals, as well as climatic and other kinds of environmental studies, provide concrete, quantifiable data—baselines against which past human patterns can be plotted. Studies of paleoecology and paleoclimate often complement archaeological studies because the relevant data sets are intermingled and inform one another. For instance, archaeological deposits often yield preserved plant and animal remains that reveal natural biotic distribution patterns as well as patterns of human exploitation (see Toolkit, volume 4). Evolutionary ecologists have developed conceptual approaches such as optimal foraging theory that archaeologists borrow and adapt with varying degrees of success.

to the key sources with which you should familiarize yourself. Many of these will be nonarchaeological sources such as historical accounts, soil surveys, ecological studies, geological guidebooks, and natural history accounts. Once again, the local and regional archaeological society publications are often the best sources for the most current work in a region. Another resource is regional research designs produced by the SHPO. These often have good overviews of work on a regional level, as well as landscape and material culture information.

Most important, spend your time in your research region wisely—keep your eyes open for opportunities to learn from knowledgeable people who live and work there. If your archaeological project em-

2.3. ETHNOLOGY TO ETHNOARCHAEOLOGY

In the heyday of culture history archaeology, most sociocultural anthropologists were primarily concerned with *ethnography,* the field study of living cultures, and *ethnology,* the comparative study of such cultures. Today sociocultural anthropology, like archaeology, is a much more diversified field, and relatively few anthropologists are interested in the kinds of questions and lines of evidence that interest most archaeologists. Yet ethnology and ethnohistory (the study of living or once-living cultures through firsthand accounts in historical documents) remain critical sources of interpretive models and tools for archaeologists seeking to understand cultural landscapes Archaeologists still make much use of the ethnographic and ethnohistoric data compiled by old-style cultural anthropologists as well as a few modern ones.

In recent decades, archaeologists have begun to conduct their own ethnographic fieldwork to focus on the dynamic links between material and behavioral aspects of living cultures. The growing subfield of ethnoarchaeology helps us explain the static archaeological record by providing "middle-range" studies of many different aspects of human behavior. While most ethnoarchaeological studies have been done by academic archaeologists, their results are equally relevant for CRM archaeologists. By looking at how living peoples generate garbage, make pottery, and survive blizzards, for example, archaeologists gain interpretive clues that help them make better inferences about the archaeological record. Such studies often show how the hot spots we call archaeological sites are but small pieces of the larger landscapes within and upon which humans live their lives.

ploys a specialist on plants, animals, or geology, make sure you are present when this expert visits. Ask questions and pay attention to what they find noteworthy about your research area. Some of your most exciting archaeological moments will come when visiting specialists share observations that help you fit together important pieces of your research puzzle. You will find that most people enjoy sharing what they know with others in informal settings, particularly if you ask good questions. And don't overlook the rancher, the landowner, and the old-timer. They may not have the scientific lingo and they may harbor folk beliefs, but most people have an innate interest in their surroundings. Experience does yield wisdom. So build rapport, show interest, and be prepared to learn from unexpected opportunities. As you become a regional expert, you'll find yourself giving back as much as you've gotten.

NAVIGATING THE POLITICAL PLAYING FIELD

The ability to navigate the political playing field for your project is a critical component of your toolkit. The world's best-planned and most significant research project cannot survive a loss of funding or a pulled permit. Academic research and CRM research navigate different waters here, but the results of political missteps are much the same. The tools you need are a good understanding of the players and their roles and how they affect your work.

The politics of the academic world are as legendary as the egos. To accomplish successful research, the academic archaeologist must placate or avoid alienating fellow professors in the department as well as various deans and university administrators, each a self-styled master of a small empire. Since much of the labor will be provided by students, the academic must also win a student following, competing with fellow professors for the best graduate students or the right to run the summer field school. Beyond the intrigue and bureaucracy of the university, academic researchers must win the support of many other players. Granting agencies and foundations operate by very different rules. To win a grant from the National Science Foundation (NSF), for instance, one has to comply with page after page of tightly worded requirements and correctly anticipate the political and theoretical biases of anonymous peer reviewers. Many private foundations have much simpler but no less precarious grant approval processes that require salesmanship of a very different sort. Cultivating foundations and wealthy individual benefactors often requires high-brow personal schmoozing and the willingness to emphasize glory and goodies over science. And even with the sabbatical, the student workforce, and the funding in hand, the academic archaeologist must still woo foreign bureaucrats, suspicious colleagues, landowners, and local officials before the first test pit can be dug. Many an academic research project has ended in ruin long before it really began because of ill-played politics on one of many different levels.

CRM archaeologists must navigate an equally strange sea. Most of the work you'll do is generated by federal laws (NHPA, NEPA, etc.; see appendix C, "The ABCs of CRM"), often administered and regulated by state agencies. You'll be working for sponsors obligated to do archaeology under these laws as well as state and occasionally local laws (see sidebar 2.4). Throw in federal and local agencies, time pressure from construction schedules, and political pressures from all levels of government, and you've got a very crowded playing field. All of these factors form the framework within which you have to do your work. Spending time learning the lay of the regulatory and political landscape can save you time, money, and heartache later. Bureaucracies are nothing if not bureaucratic, and the *i*'s you don't dot and the *t*'s you don't cross can come back and bite you on the butt. If you are going to play the game, you must learn the rules.

The first step is a basic grasp of the National Historic Preservation Act (NHPA), especially section 106 of that law and its regulations (see sidebar 2.5). Other federal laws also govern the course of sponsored archaeological research. There is a full alphabet soup of federal CRM laws, rules, and jargon (NEPA, TCP, NAGPRA, etc.) that you will encounter and need to recognize. These laws and regulations, and the way they are implemented by various federal agencies, determine when, where, why, and how archaeological research will be done and funded. This is the guts of most CRM research, and the better your understanding of the process, the better you'll be able to steer your project safely home.

One of the best ways to get up-to-date on these laws and regulations is to sign up for intensive multiday CRM training seminars and workshops. These programs are sponsored by the Advisory Council on Historic Preservation (ACHP), and various federal agencies, as well as private enterprises. The University of Nevada at Reno has developed a good reputation for offering such courses. Look for the training sessions taught by well-respected experts, especially those with experience in the agencies you'll be working with. These people can give you the no-holds-barred advice that you will need. All good training sessions, private and government sponsored, will provide you with copies of the current laws and regulations and take you through practical exercises.

In addition, reams of printed and electronic literature are put out by the federal government. The Advisory Council maintains a website with all the current federal laws, short tutorials on the section 106 process, and recent news and information on how these laws are applied (www.ACHP.gov). The National Park Service also maintains a set of excellent resources for CRM archaeologists (www.nps.gov).

Many federal regulations are administered at the state level by the SHPO and specifically by the state historic preservation officer (SHPO, also) or the deputy SHPO and his archaeology staff. Each state has developed rules or procedures to administer the section 106 process, as well as to enforce state preservation laws. It's a critical part of your toolkit to know who the players are in your state SHPO

2.4. KNOW YOUR SPONSORS

Your sponsors are the public agencies or private organizations that pay the bills for most CRM research. It's important to recognize that different sponsors have different expectations for your work. The differences in how sponsors view your work will directly affect how you handle the inevitable changes, problems, and potentials you encounter.

Public sponsors, in general, have a better understanding of the CRM laws and the process and pitfalls of CRM research than those in the private sector. Many federal and state agencies have professional staffs to coordinate this kind of research. This means that the RFPs and scopes of work you'll see from these agencies are usually fairly thorough. The staff archaeologists can usually be counted on as in-house advocates for the archaeological resource. If you encounter unexpected opportunities (say a well-preserved buried component where none was expected), these folks can often go to bat at their agencies to extend the scope of work and hopefully the budget to take advantage of these research surprises. On the downside, you may also work with sponsors who set out RFPs and scopes of work so anal and detailed that there is no room for you to apply your experience and imagination. In general, governmental sponsors are concerned with meeting the requirements of the law first, with time and money considerations following closely behind.

There are two kinds of private sponsors. The largest group consists of developers, mining companies, and construction firms that find themselves under a regulatory or contractual obligation. A smaller group consists of organizations that contract for archaeology because they have an interest in archaeology, feel that it's the right thing to do, or see the valuable public relations aspect of the work.

and how the state rules are implemented to manage the process. Many SHPOs offer seminars on the section 106 process and their state and local regulations, which is an excellent way to get up to speed on the factors that will shape your work. All SHPOs also publish guides to the state regulations and processes, and current copies should be part of your library.

One of CRM archaeology's favorite sports is SHPO bashing. Many SHPOs complain (rightly) that some archaeologists are clueless when it comes to the laws and regulations they are paid to implement. Many archaeologists complain (rightly) that the SHPO has lost touch with what's going on in the field. Most of this bashing can be attributed to miscommunication. Archaeologists need to understand that the SHPO's job is to administer and manage the federal regulatory process within the context of state government and local politics. The SHPO sees more of the archaeology done in a state than anyone else— good, bad, and ugly . . . very ugly. A little communication can go a

Sponsors who are simply fulfilling their regulatory obligations see the archaeology as a hurdle to be overcome. The budget is important, but in the context of a development project, the thing that matters most is the schedule. They usually don't have a great deal of interest in the work itself, other than getting it done on time and getting clearance to proceed. This sounds like a bad situation, but in fact it can be the basis for a very good working relationship as long as you recognize the sponsor's needs. For example, in a privately sponsored cemetery relocation, we found that a section of the ninety-year-old cemetery wasn't recorded on the plat map. The SHPO required that we locate all the burials in that area before construction could proceed. The sponsor supplied heavy equipment and operators, three-wheeled all-terrain vehicles, a professional surveyor, and laborers to help move the project forward. By working together, the sponsor was able to start his project on time, we were able to locate six additional burials, and the SHPO was satisfied.

Private sponsors who are funding the work even though it isn't required are a different case. They're often interested in what you find, and they want to feel like they've done a good thing. The budgets may be small for the work they expect, and there may also be tight schedules to maintain. The challenge for you is to work closely with the sponsors and educate them on what archaeological research really is—that it's the information that's important rather than the artifacts. Then the onus is on you to do the work in a timely manner, knowing that you probably can't expect many project extensions or budget increases. It's important to produce a well-written, readable, interesting report. These sponsors want to feel that they've made a contribution.

long way to smoothing what can be a bumpy process. Get to know your SHPO as a colleague rather than a bureaucrat to open those lines of communication. If your SHPO doesn't make regular presentations to the archaeological community, ask him or her to, and give the archaeological community at large the opportunity to interact with the SHPO.

Archaeologists working on Indian lands may need to operate under tribal laws and regulations that may take precedence over state and federal laws. Many landholding tribes now have their own Tribal Historic Preservation Office/officer (THPO), who performs the same function as the SHPO at the state level and is responsible for administering the section 106 process and applying tribal laws and regulations.

Cities, municipalities, and some counties have preservation ordinances that may control or affect research done within their boundaries. Your SHPO or THPO is generally up-to-date on local ordinances

2.5. SECTION 106 AND YOU

The National Historic Preservation Act (NHPA) of 1966 forms the cornerstone of the federal historic preservation system. Section 106 of the NHPA requires all federal agencies to take into account the effects of their actions ("undertakings") on "historic properties." The law applies to any undertakings in which federal money is spent or federal permits or licenses are issued.

The NHPA also created an independent federal agency, the Advisory Council on Historic Preservation (ACHP, usually just called the Council), to oversee the review process. The rules for the section 106 review and compliance process were developed by the Council and are published in the U.S. Code of Federal Regulations (36 CFR 800).

Under section 106, one of the first things a federal agency is supposed to do when it's going to do, fund, or permit land alteration is to see whether the proposed work will cause changes in the character or use of "historic properties" that are listed on, eligible for, or potentially eligible for the National Register of Historic Places (NRHP), including structures, objects, and districts, as well as archaeological sites. If the agency thinks that the project may affect these resources, it (or its partner state agencies or the entity that needs the permit) is required to consult with the SHPO in the relevant state or states and determine what if any kind of work needs to be done. This determination may lead to requests for proposals (RFPs) and contracts to perform surveys, testing, or mitigation. If this work finds sites that weren't previously identified or listed on the NRHP, these new sites (or new data about known sites) are evaluated

and regulations, so that is always the first place to look (good communication is paying off already!). It is increasingly common in larger cities for there to be a local preservation office that administers local preservation ordinances. Boston, for example, has its own city archaeologist and its own rules under which city-sponsored archaeology takes place.

On the archaeological side, being plugged into the grapevines that monitor federal and state politics is important to stay abreast of pending changes. At the national level, the American Cultural Resources Association's e-mail list (ACRA-L) and *The Archaeological Record* of the Society for American Archaeology (SAA) are sources where you can find current information. At the state level, check with your SHPO and make sure you receive any newsletters or publications it regularly publishes. As we've said before, join your state and regional societies. Most states also have professional organizations of CRM archaeologists; check with your SHPO to find out how to join yours.

by the agency in consultation with the SHPO. This is where determinations of eligibility and potential eligibility for the NRHP are generated.

Once a property is determined eligible, the agency works with the SHPO to determine the effect of the proposed undertaking on the property. If they determine that there will be an adverse effect, the agency again consults with the SHPO to find ways to mitigate the damage—reduce its effects. These consultations may include other "interested parties" that may be affected by the work: local governments, tribes, property owners, and preservation groups. The goal is to develop a memorandum of agreement (MOA) between the SHPO and the agency that details the work to be done to mitigate the damages to the historic properties. Federal agencies that do routine actions often strike a longer term deal with the SHPO (a programmatic agreement) that spells out and simplifies the review and compliance process. In cases where the feds and the SHPO can't agree, the Advisory Council weighs in, but ultimately the federal agency makes the call.

Archaeological contractors involved in the section 106 process are called on to perform reconnaissance, survey, or testing to determine the existence and evaluate the significance of properties within an area of potential effect (see Toolkit, volume 2). Also, you may be involved with data collection efforts designed to mitigate the effects of development on eligible properties (see Toolkit, volume 3). In either case, while the archaeological consultant is an unspoken player in the section 106 process, legal responsibility and authority for decision making falls to the federal agency and the SHPO. It requires your hard work and expertise, but they call the shots.

Every CRM archaeologist needs to know the ins and outs of section 106.

Staying current with federal, state, and local laws and regulations is always a problem. One of the best ways is to maintain an active professional network. Remain involved in professional organizations, and maintain close working relationships with your archaeological colleagues, including those who work for the sponsoring and regulating agencies. Make it part of your job to get to know the folks you'll be dealing with in the SHPO office. That way it will be easy and comfortable for you to call them when you have a question about laws, regulations, or processes. They would much rather spend a few minutes with you on the phone than have to untangle a mess six months down the road. They can also clue you in to changes in the laws and generally point you in the right direction for more information. To keep up with local practices and the political scene, there is nothing better than talking with other archaeologists. It is at meetings, brown-bag talks, and after-hours bull sessions that you'll learn more about what's happening in and out of archaeology. This advice comes directly from cultural anthropology: Be a participating observer of your profession.

As simple as this sounds, far too many CRM archaeologists have little or nothing to do with archaeology beyond what they get paid to do. It shows. Understanding the interplay between the laws and the people who administer and regulate them is critical to the successful completion of your research. The tools to deal with the political and bureaucratic landscape may not seem important when you're in the field, but when the bureaucratic crap hits the political fan, you'd better have the shovel to dig yourself and your project out. That shovel is a good understanding of the laws and the players.

WHY THE PROFESSIONAL ARCHAEOLOGIST'S TOOLKIT IS HEAVY

Sound like a lot? It is! No one should ever think that being a competent professional archaeologist is easy. The old saying "Know a man by his tools" is absolutely true. Your colleagues, regulators, and sponsors will judge you by your intellectual and practical tools and how you wield them. If you keep them sharp and well used, it will show in the quality of your work, in the way your work is received, and in the satisfaction of your sponsors. Becoming a good researcher of any stripe takes lots of training, experience, and the attitude that education is an ongoing and never-ending process.

As a professional archaeologist, realize that the tools you bring to your work shape and color the work you do and how it impacts the entire archaeological record. Just as important as your tools is how you wield them: the attitude that you bring to each project, each opportunity to explore another fragment of the archaeological record. By doing the best job you can of designing your research, you'll help make the most of each of those opportunities.

A QUICK LOOK AT THE RESEARCH PROCESS

In the broadest sense, archaeology is archaeology no matter where or by whom it is conducted. But there is no denying that North American archaeology is a two-track field: academic archaeology and CRM archaeology. There are fundamental and seemingly irreconcilable differences in the process of research in the academic and CRM worlds. In academic research, the researcher's interest (or something less noble like tenure, fame, or a convenient field school locality) is usually the genesis for a research project. In contrast, the driving force in CRM research is a sponsor's interest in completing some land-transforming construction project and a government mandate that any inconveniently situated cultural resources must be located, inventoried, evaluated, and possibly removed or excavated.

Three key differences between the research process envisioned and taught by most academic archaeologists and the one encountered in CRM archaeology are (1) the CRM process begins with a solicitation—"How much will you charge to come here and do this for me?"—instead of an initial desire or problem on the part of the researcher; (2) the CRM process has built-in, government-mandated funding mechanisms, while funding for academic research is almost always a major limiting factor; and (3) the CRM process involves legally binding contractual obligations instead of ethically binding academic promises. These fundamental differences color almost all aspects of the research process.

THE "PURE" RESEARCH PROCESS
IN ACADEMIC ARCHAEOLOGY

While academic archaeologists are sometimes viewed as high-minded scientists with a pure interest in advancing the state of knowledge, the reality is often very different. The ideal is to be able to independently develop and follow one's personal research agenda wherever it takes you. And some archaeologists have the talent, drive, good fortune, and institutional support to do just that. But most academic archaeologists take much more pragmatic routes and, like CRM archaeologists, must take advantage of research opportunities as they arise.

For pragmatic reasons, many academic archaeologists develop an interest in the archaeology of the region in which their college or university is located. It is much cheaper and logistically easier to carry out underfunded archaeological research near home than far away. And most academic research projects, near or distant, are done with budgets that pale by comparison to those in the CRM world.

Other academic archaeologists become specialists in a topical sub-field such as geoarchaeology, zooarchaeology, or archaeobotany. For most such specialists, the research process begins when they are called in as consultants to an ongoing research program. Today, many of these ongoing research programs are CRM projects. In fact, most academic archaeologists are significantly involved with CRM research at some point in their careers and many count on consulting work to supplement academic salaries and provide research funds.

Because of this diversity, it's hard to outline the "typical" academic research process. Most academically based research projects in archaeology do begin with a desire, however pure, to learn more about a topic or area. Many academics build upon research interests to which their own professors introduced them in graduate school. The ability to follow through, year after year, on a research topic or in a region is one of the greatest advantages that academic archaeologists have. CRM archaeologists have to go where the work is, while academic archaeologists can go wherever they want as long as they can solve the myriad logistical, political, and budgetary problems along the way. So let's take a real-life example involving an academically based research project that one of us (Black) took part in and look at key elements of the research process.

In the late 1970s, Thomas R. Hester from the University of Texas at San Antonio and Harry J. Shafer from Texas A&M University began a research project at a little-known Preclassic and Classic Maya center called Colha in northern Belize, a Central American country bordered by Mexico and Guatemala. Both professors were stone tool experts, lithicists, drawn to Colha because of the site's impressive evidence of large-scale stone tool manufacture. After visiting the site as part of a small conference of archaeologists interested in Maya lithics, Shafer and Hester decided to launch what ultimately evolved into a multidecade research program that is still winding down. Initially, they envisioned only a few seasons of work, but even this was a big undertaking in an underdeveloped country some 1,300 miles from home.

The first step was recognizing, articulating, and deciding to take on a research problem: Were the large mounds of chipping debris at Colha evidence of industrial-scale specialized craftsmanship? If so, when did this phenomenon arise, and what role did it play in the economy of the ancient Maya? Problem in hand, Shafer and Hester next had to figure out how they would get the money and labor to undertake the initial explorations and excavations. Luckily, Hester was acquainted with an Italian benefactor who agreed to provide a modest amount of start-up funds. The funding was stretched by attaining university support, mainly time off for Shafer and Hester, and equipment, and by involving graduate students through field schools as well as volunteers, many of them CRM archaeologists in search of an exotic field experience. Most staff members were nonsalaried and were paid only transportation costs and all the rice, beans, and canned meat product they could eat. While figuring out the funding and logistics, the lead archaeologists also had to win the permission of the archaeological authorities in Belize. Each year they negotiated a research permit that spelled out what they could and could not do and what they would do for the country, such as hire so many local workers and donate equipment. They also had to gain the cooperation of the landowners even though archaeological sites in Belize were in principle controlled by the country.

After the first few years, a serviceable field camp had been established and enough had been learned about the site to realize that much more work was needed to thoroughly address the starting problems and begin to face the many new problems that had cropped up. With private funding waning, Hester and Shafer concentrated on applying for grants from the National Endowment for the Humanities (NEH) and other granting agencies and private foundations such as the National Geographic Society and Earthwatch. Some years they succeeded in cobbling together adequate funds; some years they did not, and the field season had to be postponed a year. Each year their research designs grew more sophisticated, the research agendas more complicated, and field crews larger. While Hester administered the project, he shared the field directing duties with Shafer and several other academic archaeologists. Specialists and graduate students from their own universities and other academic institutions joined in the project, each adding his or her own research interests. Black, for instance, was a graduate student and became interested in carrying out stratigraphic excavations in the site's main plaza, an open space surrounded by small temples and elite residences.

As the work evolved, the research design was represented by many different documents, each justifying and outlining a research plan for different audiences—funding agencies, the Belizean government, graduate advisers, and field school participants. Some of the plans were carried out, others died for want of funding or because the ideas were too grandiose or otherwise flawed. Fieldwork at Colha continued intermittently into the early 1990s as new problems, new funding, new graduate students, and new field schools came along. Several graduate student veterans of the early years at Colha came back as young academic archaeologists in pursuit of their own goals. Functionally, the Colha Project was really a series of overlapping smaller research projects united by a network of personal relations linked to the lead investigators, Hester and Shafer. The results of the investigations have been presented at dozens of research conferences, academic meetings, and popular venues including a traveling museum exhibit. Numerous interim reports, journal articles, book chapters, theses, and dissertations have presented many aspects of the work, addressing the original research problems and many others that cropped up along the way. More than twenty years after the work was initiated, a final report is still in progress.

The research process in academic archaeology depends mightily on circumstance and a host of other factors that have much more to do with politics, personalities, logisitics, marketing, and the accidents of history than with the pure ideal of advancing knowledge. Although there really isn't a "normal" sequence of academic research, here are some common elements, even if they rarely happen in a neat sequence:

Problem/Opportunity → *Plan* →
Funding → *Permit* → *Work* → *Dissemination*

At Colha, after the initial opportunity and problem were defined, the other elements of the research process were repeated over and over as the research program evolved. While not all academically based research projects span twenty years, some are even longer, and most see many years between initiation and completion. While CRM projects tend to be of fixed scope and finite duration, academic projects are typically more organic, evolving, and never-ending. Whereas CRM projects almost always result in a final report, academic projects are disseminated in more diverse ways and may never culminate in the ideal outcome, a scholarly monograph.

If you are planning on becoming an academic archaeologist or if you find yourself involved in a long-term research project as a graduate student, we have two pieces of advice. The first is to carve yourself out an interesting niche that allows you to follow or develop your own interests as opposed to those of your mentor or project director. The second is to pursue finite goals and outcomes that you can reasonably expect to achieve in the time you have available. Many an academic archaeologist has gone to his or her grave leaving behind a stack of unfinished research projects and ugly holes in the archaeological record.

THE "DIRECTED" RESEARCH
PROCESS IN CRM ARCHAEOLOGY

For better and worse, the CRM world is much more cut and dried, although it, too, is very diverse. Cut to the bone, the typical contracted research process in the CRM archaeological world proceeds in five parts. It begins when an archaeological firm or organization receives a *request* from a sponsoring entity or client: "Tell us what it will take for you to solve our archaeological permitting problem." The archaeological firm replies with a *proposal:* "For so-many bucks, we will do blah-blah archaeological research work toward gaining your archaeological permit clearance." The proposal is accepted by a signed, legally binding document—a *contract*—and the archaeological firm does the *work* (field, lab, etc.) as per the contract. The process ends when the *report* is delivered to and accepted by the governmental entity that issues the permit that the client or sponsor needs. Although there are many permutations, smaller pieces, and complications, the CRM research process usually follows these five sequential parts:

Request → *Proposal* → *Contract* → *Work* → *Report*

The real world of CRM research is just as twisted and complex as the academic world, and by way of example we'll take a look at the

Wurzbach Project. In the early 1990s, the Texas Department of Transportation (TxDOT) and the city of San Antonio had decided to build a much-needed crosstown expressway—the Wurzbach Parkway—through an existing urban environment. The only practical route lay along and across the upper reaches of a major drainage system where there were stretches of undeveloped land, including what was left of an area known as the Walker Ranch, the last major holdout to urban development in north-central San Antonio. Several decades earlier, the area had been designated as the Walker Ranch Historic District and placed on the National Register of Historic Places because it contained numerous prehistoric archaeological sites as well as several historic sites, including what was left of a Spanish Colonial ranch associated with Mission San Antonio de Valero, better known today as the Alamo.

Despite the Historic District designation, the Walker Ranch area and its archaeological sites had suffered all sorts of disfiguring impacts as it was parceled up into subdivisions, paved over, and otherwise incorporated within the city. As urbanization encroached, some archaeological investigations did take place, including surveys, testing projects, and one substantial excavation. The building of a small flood control dam in the early 1980s had been preceded by the excavation of a prehistoric campsite named after the Panther Springs Creek, which it overlooked. As it happens, Black had directed that excavation and had made many of the mistakes in designing archaeological research that we are urging you to avoid. Fourteen years later, in 1993, he found himself back in the same spot because the route of the planned Wurzbach Parkway went right through Walker Ranch and what was left of the Panther Springs Creek site. Even though a last-minute shift in the dam location had spared the site from being gouged out by a footing trench, trespassing looters had churned up the site in search of chipped stone tools. But the looters had all but overlooked another, less conspicuous prehistoric campsite just across the creek, the Higgins site.

TxDOT asked Black to assemble a small research team (including Jolly) to investigate the Higgins site and several others and to evaluate their potential for continued listing on the National Register. This is section 106 talk for "Do we have to excavate the site before we blow it away?" To make a long story shorter, our team answered yes, and TxDOT entered into negotiation with the SHPO, Texas Historical Commission (THC), and the Texas Archaeological Research Laboratory (TARL) of the University of Texas at Austin where Black worked.

Because TxDOT and UT Austin were both state agencies, the request for proposals (RFPs) was not a formal document and not subject to competitive bidding. Instead, TARL presented a contract proposal that included a scope of work, a timetable, and a budget. The actual research design was developed as part of the contract and included within a technical report summarizing the results testing at the Higgins site and several others. After some negotiation, the SHPO agreed that the proposed work would constitute an acceptable mitigation program for the damage the Wurzbach Parkway would cause to the archaeological information represented at the Higgins site. Because the land was owned by the city of San Antonio, a political subdivision of the state, a Texas Antiquities Permit was also required and was issued by the THC. Shortly thereafter, the archaeological excavations that came to be known as the Higgins Experiment were under way.

By this point, several critical differences between the CRM research process and that typical of academic-based research are apparent. The process started with a looming construction project, not a burning research question. The sponsor and funding source (TxDOT on behalf of the Federal Highway Administration) sought out the archaeological research team, not the other way around. Although the researchers wrote the research plan, it was formally approved and negotiated between the sponsor (TxDOT) and the SHPO (THC), who could have altered any part of the plan without the researcher's approval. The scope of work spelled out that the work would be confined to the actual right of way of the proposed road, meaning that the research team was strictly limited to a linear research universe. Furthermore, the research timetable was relatively short (three years from start to finish) and set to accommodate the sponsor, not the researcher. Still, as CRM projects go, the researchers had a pretty free hand and a generous budget, far larger than most multiyear NSF archaeological grants.

With contract and permit in hand, we were required to start work within ninety days, and all of that time was filled with preparations. A crew was hired, and crew housing and field lab space (a portable building designated the Wurz-shack) had to be acquired and renovated. Field vehicles were scrounged and rented, computers purchased, and software written and revised for data management. TxDOT provided on-site power, a field office, and twenty-four-hour security to protect the site from both the neighborhood juvenile delinquents and the homeless vagrants who supported their drug habits by selling looted artifacts. There was also heavy equipment at

our disposal: cherry pickers for high overhead photos, a Gradall exca-
vator for pulling off overburden, and front-end loaders and large
trucks for moving dirt. The logistical support that a large agency like
TxDOT can provide is a hidden asset to many CRM projects.

The pace of the work was determined by both the budget and the
construction schedule. If we decided that we hadn't really got it quite
right the first time, there would be no option to come back in another
year or two to take a different tack. After the end of the project, construction of the Parkway—the reason that the budget, the Gradall,
and the crew were there in the first place—would destroy what we
had left of the site. Like many CRM projects, it was a one-shot deal.
We had one opportunity to use the generous resources we had been
given to make a contribution to the archaeological record. Not just a
little pressure.

The fieldwork was completed in about ninety days, and lab work
and analysis continued intermittently for another three years. The
Higgins Experiment itself was part of a larger research project covering work at several other sites, the final reports of which were issued
in a series of volumes from 1995 through 1998. Part of the work was
used by one of the consulting specialists in his dissertation work, but
no other theses or dissertations came out of the project. The results
were presented at local, state, and national archaeological meetings
but largely remain known only to a small CRM community.

The real, fundamental difference between academic research and
CRM funded research is control. In both worlds you have budgets, permits, and bureaucracies to limit and confound your well-crafted ideas.
In the academic world, though, the researcher exerts more control over
the research process. The researcher decides where and, generally,
when to work. The researcher develops the questions of interest, the
scope of work, and the research priorities. The academic researcher also
decides how and when the research results will be disseminated. In the
CRM world, many or most of these decisions are out of the researcher's
hands. The study area is prescribed by the sponsor, and the schedule is
at the mercy of funding and the construction schedule. Research questions may be designed by the researcher, but the SHPO and the sponsoring agency have the final word on what is significant and what the
research priorities will be. The sponsoring and regulating authorities
also have a large hand in determining how and when the results will be
reported, usually within a few short years or even months. It's this difference in control that is at the heart of the distinction between academic and CRM research.

The rest of this volume will focus specifically on designing research for CRM archaeology. The reality is that the vast majority of funded archaeological research in the United States is CRM archaeology. Most archaeologists will work in CRM archaeology all or part of their professional careers. To be effective, you must understand the details of how the research process really works. One steadfast rule is that from academic to CRM, from agency to agency, sponsor to sponsor, state to state, project to project, and year to year, the pieces and parts of the research process are rarely exactly the same. We will focus here, and in the rest of this volume, on the CRM side of the coin, with some quick characterizations of the most common aspects of the process that you will encounter as you design CRM research. We will follow the simplified five-part research process from start to finish, adding mention of some of the permutations you need to know about.

THE PARTS OF CRM RESEARCH

Your call to action is a request from some potential sponsor or client that has archaeological obligations. This request can begin with a simple phone call, a faxed letter of inquiry, or a formal document often called a *request for proposals* (RFP). When the sponsor is encountering the need to do archaeology for the first time, the request is usually a call or letter from someone who knows little more than what the form letter from the governmental permitting or regulating agency states: "We need a cultural resource inventory that will fulfill our obligations under section X of. . . ." The archaeologically unsophisticated sponsors do not care about the quality of the archaeological research; they are looking for a cheap, fast solution to a bureaucratic requirement. They are the most likely to go with the lowest bid and often suffer the consequences because they don't know any better. If an engineering or environmental consulting firm is contacting you on behalf of a sponsor, then your contact will be more archaeologically sophisticated and will probably have a good idea of what they are asking you to do. The engineer won't care much about the research, either, but they will want to work with competent archaeological firms that can do acceptable work in a timely fashion. For this reason, they may go sole-source (i.e., no competitive bid) and choose a reputable archaeological firm they know they can work with. If a state or federal agency is sponsoring the work, it will probably have an archaeologist or archaeologically knowledgeable contracting officer issue an RFP.

Such documents will spell out in some detail what they want and expect from you. Depending on the agency, they may pay more attention to the bottom line or to the qualifications of the firm and the responsiveness of the proposal.

The most critical part of any request, formal or informal, is the *scope of work*. As we explain in detail later in the book, the scope of work lays out what is to be done, why, when, where, and under what conditions. Naturally, you cannot design effective archaeological research in the CRM world unless you have a clear understanding of what your sponsor wants from you and of the physical, legal, and logistical research universe you will be working within. Unless you have a comprehensive RFP in hand, it will often be up to you to take what the sponsor says they want and craft a scope of work as part of your proposal.

The *proposal* is your written response to the formal or informal RFP. Proposals consist of different parts depending on the particular circumstances, but usually they contain a revised scope of work, a budget, and a schedule. The *revised scope of work* or work plan is where you say how you will address the stated scope or, in cases where the sponsor doesn't know enough to provide you with an adequate scope, where you tell the sponsor what the work will involve (i.e., you provide the scope). The *budget* tells the sponsor how much you will charge. Sometimes your budget is a fixed price for a set amount of work, and sometimes it is a cost-plus budget that says you will bill the sponsor on the basis of your actual/direct costs plus your overhead and profit margin (usually a multiplier such as 150 percent of the direct costs). The *schedule* lays out the time frame—when you will "deliver" (do) what. Formal proposals submitted to government agencies often must contain other elements that are intended to help the sponsor evaluate your proposal. For instance, you may need to provide *qualifications* such as the vitae or résumés of the key individuals who will do the work and examples of comparable work your firm has done.

Naturally, the pieces of your proposal are directly linked to the design of your research. The scope, the budget, and the schedule tightly constrain what you can and cannot do during your research. So can the qualifications and abilities of your research team. You also need to realize that in many contractual situations, your proposal may serve as the "research design." As we will keep stressing, putting the proposal together is only part of the ongoing process of designing effective research. For now, however, just keep in mind that while academic archaeologists often envision (and produce) research designs as stand-alone, formal documents (often prepared in the process of applying for competitive grants), in the CRM world the proposal often constitutes the only written research design. The smaller and more routine the work, the more likely that this is the case.

In some CRM projects the contract may call for you to prepare a formal *research design* as part of the initial stages of your work. Usually this requirement is done to satisfy the federal or state agencies that are mandating or regulating the work. Formal research designs are likely to be required in larger projects, particularly multiphase projects where many sites are involved or that involve mitigation (excavation or data recovery). In such circumstances, the research design builds on and refines the general approach outlined in your proposal. Often the research design must meet the approval of archaeological bureaucrats in state or federal agencies or both. This step can create contractual difficulties when the regulating or permitting archaeological bureaucrats demand changes that have financial consequences beyond what your budget and schedule allow (i.e., they want you to do more work than you have planned to do). If you have correctly anticipated the potential impact of the third party (the archaeological bureaucrat whose name does not appear in your two-party contract, but who plays a critical role in the outcome of your research), you have will have covered your firm's butt by inserting clauses that allow for contract modifications. (If not, you will next time!) A lot more needs to be said about the various elements that are typically involved in a formal research design, but we will save that for later.

A defining piece of the CRM research process is the *contract*. This is the signed document that legally binds the sponsor and archaeological firm or organization doing the work. In small, uncomplicated situations, the contract may be a one-page letter that says the two parties who sign on the dotted lines at the bottom of the page (i.e., the sponsor and the archaeological contractor) agree to the terms spelled out in the attached proposal. In other projects, the contract may be a lengthy document that subsumes the scope of work and the proposal (and its parts) and that spells out the contractual agreement. State and federal agencies often attach all sorts of standard clauses that cover everything from intellectual property rights to dispute resolution, safety requirements, nondiscrimination, subcontracting, and so on. In all circumstances it behooves you, the archaeological contractor (or you, the project director charged with completing the contract), to read the fine print and make sure you know what you are legally obligated to do.

You may think that with the contract signed and the research design approved, the process of designing your research project is over. This is untrue in most situations. The core of the research process is reexamining ideas and strategies as new information becomes available. As you work, you'll encounter unexpected situations, new kinds of information, and other things you didn't imagine you would encounter when you designed your research. In a perfect world, with unlimited time and money, you might be able to jot down a quick note about what you've seen and plow right ahead with your original plan, with the expectation that some time in the future you'll revisit the anomaly and attack it with its own special research plan. The reality is, though, that the work you're doing may be the last work any archaeologist gets to perform on that patch of dirt, so there is an ethical obligation to deal with unexpected circumstances as you find them. The kicker here—and one of the things that makes fieldwork fun—is that you usually can't (and shouldn't) just abandon your original plan to jump ship to some new plan for success. To do the best work you can, you need to deal intelligently with the unexpected, not by default. This means taking some time to revise or add to your research plan to handle new wrinkles. Most important of all, it means documenting—writing down—exactly what the changes are and why they're being made. If you don't document your changes, you could (rightly) be accused of misrepresenting the work that was done to fit more closely with your final conclusions. You'll be revisiting and probably revising your research plan all along the way.

THE RESEARCH PROJECT

Archaeological research projects in the CRM world come in all sizes and many different types. The stereotypical CRM project (or series of projects involving one project area) is often seen as consisting of three sequential phases, sometimes termed Phases I, II, and III. The first phase is the *survey* or *cultural resource inventory,* in which the contractor inspects the project area on foot, sinks shovel tests, and maybe some backhoe trenches. The aim is to make a reasonable effort to identify factors present in the project area (or some quantified sample of the total area) and to determine which of these are obviously insignificant and which need further work.

The next phase is *testing* or *site evaluation,* in which those identified sites that have not yet been written off (dismissed as unimportant) are looked at in more detail. The aim of testing is to determine which, if any, of the potentially significant sites are, in fact, likely to contain information that is judged to be significant by criteria such as those listed in section 106 of the National Historic Preservation Act (see sidebar 3.1).

The final phase is *mitigation* or *data recovery*, in which the sites that have survived the winnowing process—those judged to be the most significant and that will be adversely impacted by the planned actions of the sponsoring entity—are partially or (rarely) wholly excavated. The aim of data recovery is to offset or mitigate the impending impact by extracting enough data from the site so that something useful can be learned before it's too late.

Many CRM projects go through the sequential phases of archaeological research more or less as outlined. But the Phase I–III "system" is an artifact of archaeological convenience, not an immutable rule. It appears in no federal regulation. At the dawn of the twenty-first century, there are increasing numbers of projects that do not neatly fit into any of these three phases. Some agencies define "classes" instead of phases, while others stick to the descriptive labels (survey, testing, etc.). And most now recognize all sorts of permutations.

The first step might be a *literature survey* or *background research* phase in which existing records are combed for previously investigated sites, archival documentation, and research on closely comparable areas and topics. After this phase and before a full-scale survey is done, there may be a *reconnaissance* project intended to identify high- and low-probability areas so that later *intensive survey* work can be selectively directed. A fairly recent trend in projects involving large tracts of land is a *geoarchaeological* or *geomorphological evaluation*. This work is done by geologists, soil scientists, or archaeologists trained in geology. The aim is not to find archaeological sites, per se, but to understand the evolution and depositional history of the landscape in question so that the best places to find well-preserved sites or deposits of a particular age can be determined. Such evaluations often identify large areas of the landscape where little potential exists for intact, buried archaeological sites.

Similarly, testing may be broken out into several different phases of fieldwork. *Intensive testing*, for instance, may be intended to "test" a site out of existence or otherwise avoid mitigation by demonstrating that not enough remains intact to warrant a full-scale mitigation project. Or intensive testing may be done in cases where the initial testing was intended to evaluate the site but failed to obtain adequate information to plan an effective data recovery program.

3.1. WHY IS "SIGNIFICANCE" SIGNIFICANT?

You won't do CRM work for long before you confront the notion of significance. This isn't ordinary garden variety significance that we're talking about. The term has special meaning in CRM. For an archaeological site to be significant—worthy of preservation or data recovery (excavation) under section 106—it must be deemed eligible or potentially eligible for inclusion on the National Register of Historic Places. This determination is made by the federal agency in consultation with the SHPO, using your recommendations, following National Register guidelines. It's this formal significance that is significant to you.

Determining a site's significance involves two parts. First, the reviewer or the archaeologist identifies one or more "historical contexts" within which a site's significance is to be judged. Historical contexts are rationales for why the site and the information it contains are significant, but there is no commonly agreed-on definition of a historical context. It can be a broad historical theme (e.g., the late nineteenth-century western frontier), a general research problem (how did drought impact Archaic life on the Plains?), or a very narrow knowledge gap (timing of the adoption of maize agriculture in the Caddo area). Sometimes historical contexts are presented in regional or statewide research designs. They can be the research questions you've developed for your project, or they could be hypotheses developed by an academic archaeologist interested in human ecology. However they are conceived, historical contexts are used to place the site or district in perspective, to provide the reviewers with the yardstick they need to assess the site.

When you present recommendations to the SHPO or another agency for sites you think are eligible for the National Register, you should also provide suggested

Mitigation or data recovery projects also may be divided into several phases. Perhaps not enough money is available in a given funding year to excavate a large enough sample of a site, or the planned mitigation proves inadequate because of new information that comes to light. There are also *alternative mitigation* projects that may not involve data recovery at all. For instance, sometimes it is desirable to set aside a property (often one that lies outside the impact area) as an archaeological preserve in return for accepting the loss of a site within the impact area. Or maybe the effects of construction can be mitigated by covering the site in concrete or fill so it is preserved for the future. Another alternative mitigation might be preparation of a regional or topical synthesis where instead of digging up yet another example of type X site, the research team pulls together what has already been learned.

The design of your project will depend on the specific types of research that you will be expected to do. This is, of course, obvious to any experienced archaeologist, but it may not be so obvious to someone contem-

contexts for the evaluation. If there are applicable standard contexts in a regional or state research plan, use those, but you don't have to stop there. A historical context is the research design process distilled to its essence. A site can be judged under multiple contexts. This is a great opportunity to develop your research questions and build an argument for how information from a given site can illuminate these questions and deepen our understanding of the archaeological record.

Once the contexts are identified, a site is judged significant (or not) within each context with regard to one of four National Register eligibility criteria: (A) events, (B) people, (C) distinctive architectural or artistic character, or (D) information potential. Since most National Register and section 106 actions involve the built world, this accounts for criteria A through C. The vast majority of archaeological sites and districts are judged for significance under criterion D. The information potential is judged within the contexts you provide.

For a site to be significant, it must meet two requirements. First, it must contain (or likely contain) information that contributes to our understanding of human history or prehistory. Second, the information must be considered important relative to one or more historical contexts. In other words, it addresses gaps in current knowledge, informs theories that challenge or go beyond current thought, or focuses on priority areas identified by state or federal management plans.

Site significance is where your research design becomes a true management tool. The research design is a map to developing effective arguments for or against determining whether a site is significant and thus eligible for inclusion in the National Register of Historic Places. This significance determination is the critical bureaucratic step at which certain sites are consigned to oblivion and others are tagged for preservation or data recovery.

plating or beginning a career in CRM archaeology. You can't just lock in on a limited set of ways of doing archaeological research or on one set of fits-all terms. There are many different paths to doing effective archaeological research even within the confines of government mandates. We expect that the plethora of different kinds of research projects will continue to expand. Keep in mind that because archaeology is only one aspect of the wider CRM field—containing architects, historians, architectural historians, and sociocultural anthropologists, all players whose research domains may overlap with yours—interdisciplinary approaches will open new research directions.

THE RESEARCH REPORT

No matter what kind of archaeological project you undertake, your research results must be reported in some formal document.

In the vast majority of CRM projects, your report will be a technical one written by and mainly for an archaeological audience. Although archaeologists are finally beginning to break out of this rut and report their results in more creative ways to wider audiences, the technical research report is still an expected product of most projects. Your sponsor may not care, but the regulatory forces will not be satisfied with anything less for the good reason that the reporting of archaeological research is a fundamental ethical responsibility (see sidebar 3.2).

3.2. THE SIX COMMANDMENTS

Archaeological deposits are fragile, and when we excavate we destroy those deposits forever. Because we destroy what we study and because the public pays for most of our work, CRM archaeologists must follow a well-defined ethical path. Most professional archaeological societies, associations, and councils have their own codes of ethics or standards of conduct. Boiled down, most are covered by these six commandments:

Thou Shalt Not Work with Your Head Up Your Ass

You have a professional responsibility to undertake only work for which you're qualified and to do a competent job of any research project you take on. You should stretch your skills, but make sure that you have qualified people in positions of responsibility to make the critical decisions. Before you accept a project, you need to be sure that you have the people, the equipment, and the wherewithal to take it through to completion.

Thou Shalt Mind the Public's Interests

Government-mandated archaeology depends heavily on the support and interest of the public. You have an obligation to spend the public's money and its trust well and to do your best to learn something worth knowing. The public includes many groups, but you have to pay particular attention to the groups whose ancestors created the archaeological record you investigate. This means you must consult with others and do your best to reach compromises that balance the public's compelling and competing interests with your own research interests.

Thou Shalt Write Your Damn Field Notes

Your most important job in the field is to make and record accurate observations of the things you find. Once a site or portion of a site is excavated, all

Research reports come in various sizes and types. For small tasks, especially those where little or nothing of archaeological significance is found, a *letter report* may be all that is needed. These are fine if they are accessible to other researchers, but often they are filed away, and so one more set of potentially useful observations is lost for most practical purposes. Larger, multiphase research projects often issue *preliminary* or *interim reports*, which are intended to be followed by *final reports* (but too often aren't for all sorts of reasons, some of them legitimate). Sometimes projects issue reports for each phase of the

---

that is left are the bare tidbits of artifacts, some samples, and your observations of what was there. You should strive to make accurate and complete observations and measurements. After you leave, your recorded observations *are* the site.

Thou Shalt Not Sell Out the Archaeology

Don't do anything to encourage or abet those who buy and sell artifacts and loot sites. Don't offer an opinion on what an artifact might be worth (and you will be asked). Don't get involved with treasure hunting schemes and other activities that destroy the archaeological record without proper documentation. Avoid the dark side.

Thou Shalt Not Screw the Archaeology (or Your Client)

If you take a job you need to strive to complete it honestly, on time and within budget. In the real world, things don't always work out. If you suspect that you will have trouble completing the scope of work for your project, sit down with the client or sponsor and the SHPO and figure out what to do. If you're having a conflict with the client over payment, don't hold the archaeology hostage. At a minimum, do your best to properly close up the project: fill in exposed units, organize the artifacts and notes, assemble the film and photo logs, and don't obstruct any follow-up studies.

Thou Shalt Share What You Learn with Your Colleagues

Your observations and analyses gain value when they become part of the body of archaeological knowledge. The information you add to the archaeological record helps other archaeologists understand the region and evaluate sites. Your reports should be timely, and your data—notes, samples, databases, artifacts—should be available to other researchers.

work, and sometimes they combine two or more phases of work in one report. Truly massive research projects like reservoir surveys or major excavations are often reported in multivolume *report series* that might culminate with a *summary* or *synthesis* volume. Increasingly, there are also contractual requirements for *journal articles, education curricula,* and *popular accounts* in addition to the technical reports.

Before your eyes glaze over completely, consider this: *Writing your report is one of the most important aspects of designing archaeological research!* Yes, that's right—the process of designing research culminates when you complete and assess your research. Because scientific research is a cyclical and, hopefully, progressive process, it is essential that you evaluate your research design as the end of each cycle draws nigh. Otherwise, you and your colleagues are doomed to repeat your mistakes and unproductive strategies. By critically assessing both the positive and negative aspects of your research strategy, you will fulfill one of your obligations as a scientist and set the stage for the next round of research.

You might want to pause and think about the archaeological reports you have read and perhaps helped write. Is the research strategy effectively evaluated? Does the report convey the impression that the researchers made any mistakes? If not, do you think this was really the case? Finally, do you think the reader would learn anything useful from an honest and thorough evaluation?

CONCLUSION

This quick overview of the research process should point you to the places where you may need to beef up your foundation, fill in some gaps, and prepare yourself for the job at hand. Effective and successful archaeological research is a careful blend of intellect and experience. As with anything else, designing archaeological research is about what has come before—the methodological, theoretical, and practical perspectives you bring to bear on the specific research problem. Your job as a professional is to make sure that you have the knowledge and experience you need to succeed. You'll be judged both by the quality of your research and by your success at clearing bureaucratic and logistical hurdles gracefully and efficiently.

4

THE SCOPE OF WORK

The scope of work (the scope) defines the universe within which your research design, field work, lab work, analysis, and write-up will operate. It defines the limits of what you can do and sets the baseline for what must be accomplished. It outlines the time frame in which the work should be accomplished, the type of work to be done, and the products that will be delivered when the work is complete. The scope of work defines or helps you decide when you work, how many people you hire, how long you'll work, and how much work you'll be able to do. In the CRM world, the scope of work allows you to prepare a budget and response to an RFP that the sponsor will use to choose a contractor. The scope of work is where your research starts.

There is a diverse range of projects, from tiny one-day surveys to multiyear, multisite mitigation projects with budgets that some small countries might envy. The archaeological research carried out by these diverse projects differs in scope, result, and presentation. But all archaeological projects have or should have a common goal: to learn something worth knowing from the archaeological record.

Designing effective archaeological research—large, small, academic, or CRM—is a process. In the CRM world, it generally involves three essential and more or less sequential tasks. You first define and document the scope of work—when and where the work will be accomplished, why it is being done, and its logistical and legal constraints. Second, you develop and document a set of research questions and objectives—what you plan to learn from the work. Third, you figure out your methodology and research strategy—how you will collect and analyze the data you need to address your research questions. It's only after this third step that you actually have a real research design—a complete plan of action.

The same three elements are equally critical in academic research. In the academic world, the process of designing research usually begins by posing research questions because it's the researcher's initiative or an opportunity that drives the process, not that of an external sponsor. The research strategy and methodology often come next. The scope of work may not be worked out until many months (or even years) later once you know how much money and labor you can muster.

The scope of work is the place to map out the things that will define and limit your research universe. The scope determines where on the landscape you'll work and the basic parameters of what you will do (i.e., survey, testing, mitigation, etc.). Vague scopes of work may do little else. Comprehensive scopes may specify when you'll work, how long you'll work, and how much work you will do. Scopes written by an archaeological bureaucrat with very specific expectations may go as far as spelling out how many samples you will take, what methodology you will follow, and what research problems you are to address. More typically, the scope of work will set minimum expectations and ask you to follow a set of guidelines or standards developed by your SHPO or other archaeological organization, such as your state's archaeological council.

In CRM research, the scope may be prepared by your sponsor. It might be vague and amorphous and might even ask for the impossible—survey and test sites on 1,200 acres of prime archaeological ground within the next two weeks. When a scope of work is prepared by the sponsor, it could be the work of an engineer or manager who simply doesn't understand what's involved in the CRM aspect of her project. Her interest may be with the time line and the budget, not the archaeology. Or the scope of work might not even physically exist. It might be simply a phone call or meeting where the sponsor lays out what needs to be done to fulfill its requirements under the law and to keep its project on time and on budget.

Regardless of what the sponsor provides as a scope of work, your first task is to thoroughly understand and document the parameters—the scope—of the work to be done. If a written scope is provided, you will likely need to talk with the sponsor to clarify anything that is unclear and make sure that you and the sponsor are on the same page regarding the work to be accomplished and the time frame involved. In a competitive bid situation, agency or state bidding rules may not allow you and the sponsor to meet and clarify issues in the scope of work. In that case, you're the one who must make the decision, but it is doubly critical that you explicitly define *in writing* the assumptions you're making about the scope of work. If you're awarded the contract, the first item of business should be a memo to the sponsor outlining your understanding of the scope of work and listing any issues that should be resolved and documented in writing.

If a written scope of work does not exist, it is your job as an archaeological researcher to create one. It should be written down, as a memo, a letter, a part of a formal contract—something you can share with the sponsor, regulators, or grantors so everyone is literally reading from the same page. If a sponsor gives you the scope of work over the phone or in a meeting, create a memo reiterating what you talked about and send it to him. If there is simply no scope of work, create one with what information you have using your best archaeological judgment. Without a real written document, you, your research design, and the success of your entire project are at the mercy of notoriously fallible human memory. Get it down on paper: dated, signed, and delivered.

If you're new to creating scopes of work or even if you've been doing it for years, the first place to start is with your SHPO office. The folks there see more scopes of work in a year than most of us will see in a lifetime. Because they often have the opportunity and responsibility to follow these projects from start to finish, they have seen what works and what doesn't. They're as busy as the rest of us, so don't expect a half-day seminar on what a good scope of work looks like, but a quick phone call might shake loose a couple of examples of the kinds of scopes of work that they're seeing from your area. This will be a much smoother process if you have invested the time to develop a good working relationship with your SHPO. The SHPO office is an underutilized research resource in most states, and you should take advantage of their expertise. A comprehensive scope of work is to everybody's advantage.

To develop a good scope of work, you need to focus on six primary areas: the project area, the work, work standards, time frame, budget, and logistics. First, critically read and understand what material you already have in hand. If it's in your head, write it down. Then read it through and mark sections that are unclear or for which you need more information. If there are any missing sections, note them, and sketch out the information you need to complete them. For example, if the work involves excavation of sites that can be reached only by boat, will the sponsor provide transportation to and from the site area? Will you need permits to perform water screening in a public waterway? Does the schedule allow for lost time over holidays or bad weather? Where you have questions or need more information, talk with the sponsor if possible and document the answers (or lack thereof) so that you and your sponsor have a clear understanding of the project area, the work to be done, the work standards to be applied, the time frame for completing the project, the project budget, and any special logistical problems or needs.

THE PROJECT AREA

This is the physical place where the work will take place—not the approximate location, but the exact boundaries of the property where the work is to be done. In the section 106 process, one has to deal with the area of potential effect (APE), which is supposed to include all areas that will be affected directly and indirectly by the proposed project. Some agencies take a much narrower view than others. Usually the project area (and APE) is depicted on one or more maps that outline the project boundaries. If some work has already been conducted in the area, the maps may show identified site locations, or it may be up to you to determine whether previously recorded sites exist within the project area. This seems pretty obvious, but if your idea of the project area isn't exactly the same as your sponsor's, you could be doing unnecessary—possibly illegal—work or leave work undone that needs to be completed. From a research perspective, the most basic research questions focus on the landscape: If it is unclear where you'll do your work, your research will be unfocused. From the contractual perspective, poorly defined project areas are red flags that alert the experienced archaeologist that he may be in for some very ugly and possibly costly surprises. Pin it down.

Keep in mind that the neatly bounded areas marked on your project map may be difficult or impossible to accurately locate on the ground. How will the project boundaries be marked? Who is responsible for marking them? Will the sponsor provide a surveyor to mark boundaries and establish a permanent datum, or will this be your responsibility? If you're not familiar with the area, it's a good idea to get input on the actual conditions on the ground. The thirty-year-old U.S. Geological Survey quad map or five-year-old U.S. Department of Agriculture air photo may show a nice clear terrace slope for your survey. If there is actually a hundred-acre bramble patch there, you will be in for a very thorny surprise. These kinds of easily overlooked details can make a big difference in your budget and schedule.

THE WORK

Knowing exactly what work is expected is a critical component of the proposed scope. What needs to be done archaeologically? Where along the CRM continuum does the project fall? Is it a survey project, testing, data collection, or some combination thereof? Are there other cultural resources to be dealt with in addition to the archaeological ones? Will you be expected to carry out nonarchaeological tasks such as archival research, oral history, or architectural documentation? With what federal and state laws and regulations will the work need to comply? What specifically will you be contractually obligated to do? You need to understand exactly what is expected and work to clarify anything that is unclear.

You also need to make sure the scope of work is understood and accepted by all of the critical players involved. The sponsor may have no real idea what it is asking you to do and what the regulators require, and it may expect you to perform miracles for less than $10,000. The regulators may not know what you have contracted to do. It could fall to you to educate the sponsor and inform the regulators (see sidebar 4.1). It's in your interest to make sure everybody is on the same page by writing or rewriting the scope of work and getting it into the hands of those who need to know.

Watch out for overly rigid specifications that assume a perfect world. On a fairly large-scale testing project in the Southwest, the scope of work prepared by a federal agency required excavation of a particular volume of soil. Unfortunately, the project area consisted of deflated terraces and hill slopes where the soil depth reached a maximum of five to ten centimeters, and there simply wasn't that much soil to be excavated from the sites tested. With a few weeks left to complete the project, the archaeological contractor made the decision to trench through portions of a site simply to increase the soil volume moved to meet the scope of work. Nothing archaeologically was learned from the trenching, and while the site was deflated, that portion of it was destroyed because they had not taken the time to understand the character of the project area or to question the work that was required in the scope.

4.1. AVOIDING THE VICIOUS REGULATORY CYCLE

An all too familiar and very unhappy pattern can characterize CRM projects: The sponsor does not know what the regulators expect. The regulators don't know what the sponsor is having its archaeological contractors do. The unethical contractor plays both ends to fatten his middle. He accepts a contract from the sponsor to do what he knows the regulators will consider inadequate work. He does the work, milks every possible dime from the sponsor, files his report, and waits for the regulators to raise objections. The regulators review the report and call for more work. The sponsor is forced to shell out more dollars to the contractor who pretends to be outraged by the evil and unfathomable SHPO or federal or state agency. The sponsor calls the SHPO and screams bloody murder. The SHPO tries to explain the requirements and points out that the contractor should have been aware of these (in a nice way because most SHPOs are too politically attuned to call a crook a crook). The sponsor is confused but finds it easier to blame the governmental regulator than the kiss-ass contractor, who swears loyalty to the client. In extreme cases, the sponsor calls his legislators and demands that they lean on the regulatory agency. In a recent case we witnessed, this vicious cycle resulted in the SHPO's office having to finish the archaeological work out of state-appropriated funds.

Guess who loses in all this? Everybody except the unethical contractor who moves on to the next unsuspecting client. The archaeological record gets the shaft. So does the archaeological profession. We all suffer for the sins of our unethical colleagues. The sponsoring and regulatory worlds grow distrustful of archaeological contractors. If enough powerful people become involved, preservation laws and regulations can be weakened.

You can avoid this vicious cycle by being an ethical archaeologist. Educate your sponsor right from the get-go and let her know what the regulators expect. You've been hired for your expertise—demonstrate it. Head off conflicts and problems by talking with your sponsors and regulators on a regular basis. If you see a problem on the horizon, get on the phone, send a fax, shoot an e-mail, or wave your semaphore flags. The single best way to head off conflict and contention is to communicate effectively. If conflict does loom, do your best to be up-front and honest with all the parties and get problems resolved early on.

You can also help by becoming a registered professional archaeologist (RPA) and living by the register's Code of Conduct, a set of standards that states, among other things, that an RPA will not "engage in conduct involving dishonesty, fraud, deceit or misrepresentation about archaeological matters." The American Cultural Resources Association (ACRA) also has a strong Code of Ethics, and you can expect CRM firms that are members of ACRA to be reputable places to work.

If the scope calls for excavation of so-many cubic meters, are there provisions for modifying the scope if something especially time-consuming (e.g., unexpected burials) is encountered? How about allowances for bad weather? These and other factors can prevent your team from being able to complete the scope of work. You can protect your interests by asking the sponsor to modify the scope of work or by spelling out contingencies in your proposal and outlining how such difficulties will be resolved.

WORK STANDARDS

To what standards will your work have to measure up? A comprehensive scope will probably specify that your work (and the qualifications of your key team members) must past muster with relevant federal and state requirements or professional standards. You may also be expected to follow the established or mandated practices in the region. These can take the form of published standards or guidelines, or they may be less formal, but no less real, unwritten expectations on the part of the regulators. If your sponsor does not understand these standards and expectations, you should carefully explain them because they often affect schedules and budgets. Pointing these out up front may help the sponsor realize that your more costly bid is a better deal than the cheaper (and competing) one that does not purport to meet standards.

TIME

In most cases, CRM contracts are designed to run for a specific length of time. The project time span determines to a large extent the size of the budget you'll have and how much work you'll be able to do. Time is highly correlated with money. The kinds of methods you can use in the field are controlled to a large extent by the time–money relationship. You may intend to water-screen every bucket of dirt through 1/8-inch mesh with deionized water, but if you've got only six weeks to test a dozen sites, that's not bloody likely.

In many areas of the world, weather plays a big factor in determining when fieldwork can be done and how long it will take. Make sure the scope of work will not have you trying to excavate in frozen earth (or, if so, that you have budgeted and planned accordingly). Surface surveying is largely a waste of time when the ground is covered in snow, mud, or seasonally thick vegetation. Your sponsor may not realize this and may need to be educated. In the CRM world, fieldwork rarely seems to take place during the optimal times of the year despite the best laid plans. Play it smart and plan for this by adding contractual clauses that modify the scope of work (and/or the budget) if predictable (or unpredictable) climatic or seasonal conditions occur that adversely affect your work.

MONEY

Few formal scopes of work spell out the amount of money that will be spent—it is your job to propose to do the specified work for a price you set. But often the sponsor has a budgeted or otherwise restricted amount of money to spend on archaeology. You may be told something like "I sure hope you can do this work for under $20,000; that's all we have." Or you may become aware of financial limits through less direct means. However it happens, the cost of doing a given project is directly related to the scope of work. The more you are asked to do, the more demanding the logistical conditions are, the more rigid the work standards—the more it will cost to do the work. Money, of course, also comes into play in competitive bidding.

Much CRM work today is contracted through competitive bidding. Ideally, the bids will come from ethical and competent companies that are all bidding on the same scope of work. The price differences should reflect differences in experience, efficiency, labor-unit costs, overhead, innovation, and concern for profit. But in the real world, the playing field is often uneven, and competing firms use a variety of strategies to win bids. Some may calculate what they think the sponsor is willing to pay and bid no more, even if it is not enough to do the work properly. Others may calculate what their competitors will bid and set their own price lower. Still others may be inexperienced contractors who tender unrealistically low bids based on little more than wild guesses. All of these tactics sometimes win contracts, but often the archaeological record suffers as a result of significantly underbidding the cost of doing a good job.

For the ethical bidder the only reasonable approach is to do your best to calculate the true costs of successfully addressing the scope of work (see sidebar 4.2). There is no adequate substitute for experience. Experienced archaeological contractors who carefully manage their projects can usually predict about what it will actually cost to do a set amount of work under known conditions. They also know what contingencies to allow for and what fatal flaws to be on the lookout for. Such individuals will read a scope of work very carefully and may not elect to bid on poorly or unrealistically conceived projects.

LOGISTICS

Scopes of work may spell out (or fail to spell out) other logistical provisions that will directly affect your ability to do the work in a timely and cost-effective manner. A prime example is access: Who owns the land, and who controls access? While this may not be an issue with many CRM projects, it can be a real problem when private landowners are involved or when more than one party controls access to the property. Make sure the scope of work spells out who will provide access and what conditions are involved. Usually it is the responsibility of the sponsor to secure access, but not always. We have experienced costly delays when access issues have cropped up at the last moment—the crew is twiddling thumbs and drawing per diem, rented vehicles sit idle, and contractual obligations loom. Cover yourself on this one; make sure you have contractual provisions that protect you in the event that access problems arise.

Another logistical consideration is whether heavy machinery or other specialized pieces of equipment are needed. The scope of work and/or the contract should spell out who provides what. If the sponsor says it will provide all the needed equipment, you should make sure that this is written down, again so that you're covered.

Images of heavy machinery and covering yourself conjure up another thing you need to consider: Occupational Safety and Health Administration (OSHA) regulations, especially those regarding trench safety (see sidebar 4.3). Traditionally, archaeologists have been lax, but the CRM world is becoming increasingly aware that OSHA safety regulations apply to archaeological work. This is particularly true in trenching and deep excavations. Planning safe excavations is always important, even though meeting OSHA requirements may go far beyond what you consider safe. You need to educate yourself about these requirements and the logistical consequences of following OSHA standards. Such considerations may well alter your research design and significantly impact your budget.

4.2. HOW MUCH IS TOO LITTLE?

Underbidding a project is bad—on several fronts. The most obvious problem is that you'll run out of money before the work is finished. You may end up with boxes of materials in your garage that you've obligated yourself to analyze. You may have an unfinished report dangling over your head and dropping into your lap every time you think you've got a little slack. Aside from the personal angst of leaving a job unfinished, you could also jeopardize your ability to get new contracts or the required permits for new projects.

We archaeologists have a stewardship responsibility to the archaeological deposits that we disturb. When we destroy a deposit via backhoe trenches, excavation units, test pits, shovel tests, surface collecting, or any other destructive technique, we have an absolute obligation to systematically record all relevant observations, curate the collected material properly, and analyze and report on the materials recovered. The only way to fulfill your obligation to yourself, the regulations, and the archaeological record is to complete your work.

Here are a few tips on how to avoid underestimating the money required to fulfill a scope of work:

1. Unless you know the general project area from firsthand experience, try to take a quick trip there and see the lay of the land for yourself. Failing that, do some homework and read up on work that others have done nearby. Consult with people who are experienced in the area. This effort may be more than rewarded by preventing you from badly misjudging the logistics of working in an unfamiliar area.

CONCLUSION

Once you've worked through your scope and satisfied yourself that all the bases have been covered, you've started the process of designing effective archaeological research. The purpose of the scope of work is to make sure that everyone involved—you, your sponsor, the regulators, interested parties, everyone—has the same understanding of what is to be done, where, and when. It may be that you share your revised scope of work with the sponsor as part of the bidding process and submit it as part of your proposal. Or in more informal situations, it may be enough to fax over a copy and discuss the revisions and additions over the

2. If you don't know what it will cost to do a given set of work, find out. Call on someone who is experienced, and ask for help. Hire an experienced hand to help you. Beg if you have to, but get help before it is too late. Once your proposal has been accepted and you have signed a contract, you are stuck with your bid.

3. If you have to guess, guess high. This may lessen your chances of getting the work, but if you land it, you'll have a better chance of breaking even or making a profit.

4. Word your proposal and contract carefully to acknowledge and allow for as many contingencies as possible. If possible, give yourself some wiggle room, so you can make adjustments when reality rears its ugly head. One way to do this is to prioritize your research plan and distinguish between "must do" and "intend to do (if all goes well)" items. Make sure the contract obligates you only to complete the "must do" list.

5. If you do fail to accurately estimate the cost of doing everything the scope of work calls for and you find yourself in a rapidly deteriorating circumstance (the money is running out, and there is lots of work still to do), the best policy is honesty. Go to your sponsor and explain what happened as soon as you possibly can—you screwed up, or, less judgmentally, you were dealt an unexpected hand by nature or the archaeological record. Try to renegotiate the contract or scope. Your sponsor may or may not be willing to give you a break, but cutting needed corners, lying, and other forms of deceit are sure paths to archaeological perdition. If all you care about is making a buck, why not pick a more profitable line of work?

phone. Expect some negotiation as part of this process. Remember that time is more precious than money to many sponsors. If your project is part of the environmental review process for a major development or construction project, the schedules for contracted work can extend over half a decade or more. Be prepared to be flexible where you can and hard-nosed where the research is concerned.

4.3. OH, MY GOSH, IT'S OSHA!

OSHA, the Occupational Safety and Health Administration (www.osha.gov), is concerned with your and your crew's safety, even if you aren't. Plus, OSHA is equipped with the clout to make you become concerned, to make you take action to protect your workers, and to shut your project down dead. But OSHA is nothing to be scared of if you do your homework and follow the rules as closely as you can.

You'll most likely encounter OSHA regulations and their strict enforcement when you're working on a project for a federal agency or a large state agency that gets most of its money from the feds, like our various state departments of transportation. While OSHA has enforcement responsibility for any business with more than one employee, the odds are against ever encountering an OSHA inspector in the wild. It's much more likely that you'll come up against an agency or corporate safety officer. Their job is to make sure that the folks working for them—including contractors—obey OSHA regulations to head off possible lawsuits.

While there are literally tens of thousands of pages of OSHA safety regulations, most archaeologists encounter problems only when we start to trench (i.e., excavate deeply) or use heavy equipment. Before heading to the field, you need to check on the possible location of any utility lines or pipes. This may not be a big deal in the wild yonder, but it only takes one nick in a high-voltage cable to ruin your backhoe operator's whole day. Many states and utility companies have a central hot line for utility line location. The companies will flag any lines in your project area for free within a few days of your call. Call before you dig! When trenching, you need to ensure that there are no surface hazards in the way of the trench. Another common-sense rule is that no employees can be under the backhoe bucket. Nor should anyone be near the area where the excavated material is dumped (unlike one of our favorite crew chiefs who liked to have us hold the wheelbarrow while he tried to dump a backhoe bucketful of dirt into it). Make sure anyone in the trench is wearing an approved hardhat and that all equipment and vehicles remain more than two feet from the edge of the excavation so stuff doesn't fall on the heads of the folks in the trench.

If you do plan to trench, and you expect that your trenches will be deeper than five feet (1.5 meters), you'll be responsible for developing a plan to slope or bench the sides of the trench or to install shoring to protect folks from cave-in. Trench collapses aren't accidents—they are manifestations of physics and soil mechanics. The exact formula for benching or sloping or shoring depends on the soil type and projected depth of the trench. The regulations require that these calculations be made by a registered engineer or other competent person. Your best bet in these situations, and really any time you work for a large agency, is to contact the agency's safety officer and get his input on the planned work. Don't guess: Ask the experts or get the OSHA training yourself. If you plan to do much trenching more than 1.5 meters deep, be sure to ask your sponsor about meeting OSHA regulations when you are preparing your proposal. Renting shoring systems or benching an excavation can radically change the schedule and budget for what you might assume would be a simple stratigraphic trench or excavation block.

Most OSHA regulations are common sense and are there for your safety. The simplest and best way to handle site safety is like everything else: Plan for it. Take an OSHA short course. If your sponsor or company has a safety officer who works with contractors, contact her, get her input, and take it to heart. For the slight inconvenience it might be to wear that hardhat on a hot day, it's a lot hotter with a metal plate in your head.

5

RESEARCH QUESTIONS

The research questions you pose and attempt to tackle will form the core of your research plan. If you are able to frame good research questions, you'll be much more likely to learn something worth knowing. Conversely, if your questions are vague or purely technical in nature ("Are there sites here?"), the odds are slim that you will actually be doing much research. You really can't do any kind of research without asking good questions.

Research questions, problems, and hypotheses are essentially the same thing. You may prefer to structure your research in terms of problems to be solved or addressed or hypotheses to be tested. Or you might start with a grand, overarching problem or hypothesis and break this down into narrower questions or sets of expectations and test implications. It really doesn't matter what you call them. What matters is that you develop and articulate clear, structured ideas about what you are trying to learn, so that your research strategy will be focused and aimed at acquiring specific sets of information that will inform your research questions, problems, or hypotheses.

No matter what you call them, research questions are simply what you plan to learn about the archaeological record. As all archaeologists know, you may not learn what you want to from your archaeological work. You may learn other things, or you may disprove something you set out to prove. If your mind is fully engaged, you will always end up with more new questions than definitive answers. But by planning to learn something worthwhile, you're focusing your work, focusing your approach on something concrete. Such strategic planning is the essence of all science—no less so for archaeology done to satisfy government requirements. If archaeologists are to continue to suckle the CRM teat in the twenty-first century, we sure better be learning things worth knowing. So a research question is really the core of a plan for learning.

In many cases in CRM, particularly those involving small, routine projects, the scope of work in your proposal may be as far as your formal research design goes. Even so, you need to elaborate the work portion of your scope and develop some explicit research questions. Otherwise, you are not really doing archaeological research—you are just performing a technical service that has comparatively little chance of making a meaningful contribution beyond the most basic site records. It's the difference between going through the motions and doing archaeology with your mind fully engaged. Often, the choice is yours.

Over and over we've observed colleagues who just "shovel it out and write it up," who often lack basic research skills, and who make little or no effort to keep current (which is easy to tell since they can't hold up their end of a research conversation with a two-by-four). They may be perfectly nice people, but they wouldn't know an interesting research question if they stepped on it. And not surprisingly, most of their "research" questions are seldom more profound than "How much can I get away with charging my client to dig these holes?" Conversely, our colleagues who are well prepared, involved in their research, and in tune with what's current are blazing productive trails into the archaeological record. These are the folks who everyone wants to talk to at the annual meeting, who everybody wants on their research team, and who rarely have trouble getting their research designs and draft reports accepted. These are the real archaeologists, the ones who embrace CRM as an opportunity for doing research.

Most research questions are posed to address holes in current archaeological knowledge. CRM research often begins with very basic and mundane holes: Are there any sites in this previously unexamined area? How old are they? What time periods and archaeological cultures do they represent? What are the depositional circumstances and preservation conditions? Has the site's recent history left enough traces of its ancient history intact to warrant more archaeological investigation? As work progresses from survey and preliminary testing, holes begin to emerge that are potentially more profound. Does this Paleoindian site preserve the data needed to shed light on the mobility patterns of Clovis peoples? Can this ruined nineteenth-century textile mill tell us something worth knowing about the Industrial Revolution in New England?

Your research questions will be framed within many contexts. Your approach to doing archaeology, the type of project, the nature of the project area, and even the folks who are on your crew will determine the kinds of questions you can ask and the kinds of results you can expect. To start developing your research questions, you need to understand these contexts and how they interrelate. At the base of everything you do is the approach you take to archaeological research.

TYPICAL APPROACHES TO ARCHAEOLOGICAL RESEARCH

While archaeologists often conceive of themselves as eclectic scientists, most tend to follow a narrow path from one research project to the next. Here we contrast four typical approaches and consider their impact on designing research. Keep in mind that ideas and attitudes are rarely exclusive to one approach or another. The first two approaches, scientific archaeology and culture history archaeology, are common to both academic and CRM archaeology. The second two, compliance and management archaeology and archaeology-as-business, are unique to CRM, although some academic archaeologists participate in these approaches as well.

SCIENTIFIC ARCHAEOLOGY

Much verbiage has been expended debating what archaeology as a science is and how it should proceed. As we alluded to in the introduction, we like the simple dictum: "Science is a strategy for learning." Pressed for a label, most academic archaeologists in North America call themselves processualists or cultural ecologists. Processualists consider themselves to be scientists engaged in research aimed at understanding the cultural processes by which human societies evolve and adapt. Cultural ecologists also consider themselves to be scientists but focus on the dynamic interaction between human societies and their environments. While archaeologists, postprocessualists also employ other scientific strategies (and may prefer to call themselves evolutionists or various other kinds of -ists), these have in common the goal of developing bodies of knowledge based on systematic observation, experimentation (or repeated sampling), and evaluation. A well-considered research design is fundamental to all scientific approaches because it lays out one's research problems and links these to method and theory. Yet scientific archaeological research designs can be densely written documents in which buzzwords, rhetoric, grand ideas, and abstract concepts take precedence over pragmatics. Done well, a scientific approach highlights explicit research questions or hypotheses to be tested and evaluated through a formal and achievable process. As should be obvious by now, we think a scientific approach is critical for the success of all substantive archaeological research projects, including those in the CRM world.

CULTURE HISTORY ARCHAEOLOGY

Archaeologists of almost any stripe share a common need to place archaeological finds in time and space. Prior to the 1960s, most American archaeologists thought of themselves as (pre)historians bent on reconstructing past cultures and past events. While the culture history approach is no longer the discipline's central focus, it still provides the basic chronological framework and nomenclature that most explanations about the human past require. Although these days few academic archaeologists younger than age fifty champion culture history as a productive strategy for learning, most archaeologists still follow field traditions that were developed to address basic cultural-historical problems.

The best culture historians have an enviable command of the ethnographic and archaeological record and often take a detectivistic and functional research approach aimed at reconstructing the human history of particular areas and tracing broader patterns of human behavior. "Typical" culture historians emphasize categorization, description, and chronology following the premise that once enough details are amassed, clear patterns and truths will emerge. This enduring sort of blind empiricism and typological wallow is not a viable part of any real science, and it was never the culture historian's ultimate goal. Today many CRM research designs continue to focus on traditional cultural-historical goals such as refining chronology and studying little-known cultural periods and regions. When linked to more robust scientific frameworks, such goals can be fruitful, but as ends in themselves, they often contribute little to an improved understanding of the archaeological record.

COMPLIANCE AND MANAGEMENT

In archaeology, like any arena in which government is involved, the process of following, implementing, and monitoring regulations has taken on a life of its own. Curse them if you will, but bureaucracies have their own logic, a logic embodied by the term *cultural resource management.* Instead of learning about the human past, the prime directive is to comply with the legal and bureaucratic mandates and manage culture resources, of which archaeological sites are only one category. Government archaeologists often prepare the scopes of work and requests for proposals that contracting archaeologists respond to. The language of section 106 has become the lingua franca of CRM research.

Excellent archaeological research can be accomplished much more easily within the framework of compliance and management when you learn to how to couch your research strategy in terms of the bureaucratic process. The downside, of course, is that satisfying the process often becomes the sole objective rather than the means by which worthwhile research is accomplished. Without linkage to scientific objectives, compliance and management research designs are often incredibly boring and nonproductive exercises in government excess.

ARCHAEOLOGY-AS-BUSINESS

Over the past twenty-five years, the epicenter of archaeological research has shifted from the university to private enterprise. The positive side is that for-profit firms have brought more efficient business practices to an inefficient discipline. Private companies can respond quickly to the changing contexts, client needs, and deadlines of government-mandated archaeology. The best consulting firms employ well-trained archaeologists and specialists in other fields who are committed to achieving meaningful and cost-effective research within a viable business environment. The downside is epitomized by low-bid "archaeologists" whose main goal and chief skill are exploiting the process for their own profit. Such unethical individuals and firms survive largely because the discipline has not yet figured out how to effectively regulate itself as a profession. In designing archaeological research, a businesslike approach forces you to look closely at the true costs of a research plan. When business and science are appropriately linked, excellent research can result. When the linkage is weak or absent, archaeology-as-business utterly fails as a worthwhile research endeavor.

LANDSCAPE: A CROSS-CUTTING APPROACH

All approaches to archaeological research share a common need to understand the physical, ecological, and cultural landscapes within which we find the patterns we study. Understanding these contexts, and the processes that shape them, is at the core of all archaeological research, no matter its theoretical, political, or bureaucratic focus. Without these contexts, field research is a mindlessly routine mechanical process.

The landscape provides the real-world context for the things we study. A landscape approach is not an alternative to scientific archaeology (indeed, it's critical to cultural ecology) or to one of the other typical approaches we outlined but is a necessary and integral element of most productive archaeological research projects. This is especially true of CRM projects that seek to evaluate and make life-and-death judgments about small, arbitrary segments of the surviving in-the-ground archaeological record. Few intelligent management and research decisions are possible unless they are informed by a keen appreciation of the wider landscapes to which all cultural resources belong. You literally have to know the lay of the land and its culture history, depositional environments, and paleoecology to make an informed judgment about the information potential of a newly tested or discovered site.

Landscapes are defined and understood through studying the distributions and interactions of plants and animals; the geological processes and formations on and within which plant and animal communities exist; the climatic regimes that govern geological and biological processes; and the land use patterns of modern, historic, and prehistoric peoples. Developing an understanding of these interrelated landscape contexts is a key part of any archaeological study. With a clear understanding of the local landscape, an archaeological team is able to devise intelligent and productive research strategies. The key here is *team*.

Successful landscape studies are usually accomplished by archaeological research teams that include experts in diverse fields such as geology, soils, geography, botany, and zoology, among others. Some are archaeologists who have developed specialties, while others are specialists from other fields. The composition of your team will vary greatly, of course, depending on the research circumstances. For instance, when undertaking research in unknown or poorly known territory, many archaeological projects today employ geologists, soil scientists, or geoarchaeologists whose task it is to study the physical landscape before them and figure out how it formed and changed during the time spans in which humans may have used it. Archaeologists are often able to draw on existing studies made by botanists, paleontologists, hydrologists, and many other kinds of scientists whose research interests conveniently intersect with those of archaeology.

In taking a landscape approach, archaeologists are often able to focus research effort on the landscape contexts themselves. Obviously in an archaeological research project the emphasis is on understanding or exploring the archaeology of the study area. But by recognizing and targeting important depositional and environmental data, we can place our archaeological data in more meaningful contexts. Such an approach helps ensure that every project, no matter how small or seemingly insignificant, can make a contribution to our knowledge of the archaeological record. If we focus only on archaeological aspects of our research, then a survey that finds no sites could be (and often is) considered a waste of time. The same survey, though, is an opportunity to document a small part of the landscape and add to our overall understanding of the region. Such information informs future research.

The contexts of archaeological site deposits are too complex and too varied for us to depend on the random interest of other professionals for the data we need. A landscape approach allows archaeologists to take the lead in developing the rich contexts we need to usefully study archaeological deposits. By broadening our reach, we can ensure that our work is useful and interesting.

DEVELOPING YOUR OWN APPROACH

Quite likely your own approach to archaeological research will be only partially under your control, unless you own a consulting company or have marched far enough up the career ladder so that you are calling the shots. Even then, the contexts in which you are doing research will determine many aspects of your approach. It is your choice either to blindly follow the pack to do archaeology by default or to approach your archaeology actively and creatively.

Developing your own approach is something you will work on most of your career. Early on you'll be told what to do as you experience the shock of trying to reconcile the archaeology you learned in college with the archaeology you encounter in the trenches and offices of the CRM world. Your idealistic mind asks, What the heck is scientific about digging shovel tests day in, day out? And what does coming in under budget so the company can make a profit have to do with doing research? Lots of would-be archaeologists never make it beyond this point and quit in disgust or disillusion. Others abandon their academic ideals and learn to walk the CRM walk without thinking much about the connection between what they do and the scientific goals of the archaeological discipline. But many of us carry on the struggle as our careers unfold. We see things that work and things that don't, opportunities that pay off and those that are squandered, and we vow to do our best when our turn comes to make decisions.

It's up to you to develop your own approach and do your best to find ways of achieving meaningful archaeological research within the contexts and confines of the CRM world. Your own approach will evolve from its idealistic and naïve beginnings as you mature and gain experience. If your commitment to the discipline of archaeology stays strong, you will figure out how to reconcile theory with practice and craft an approach that works for you and your situation. You will see that a pure scientific approach is difficult, if not impossible, to follow in CRM but that scientific goals can be pursued and reconciled with compliance, management, and business goals. You will also see how hard yet essential it is to understand the past landscape contexts within which lived the people who created the archaeological remains you study.

The approach you take to archaeological research will probably suggest to you several relevant research questions for just about any project. If you're interested in culture history, filling gaps in a regional chronology might be a likely question. If compliance needs loom large, you're probably asking basic questions like site location and condition. If you take a scientific landscape approach, you may be more interested in the evolutionary relationships between climate and social complexity in your region. Whatever your approach, whatever the scale of your project, you'll need to develop a guiding set of research questions.

CREATING RESEARCH QUESTIONS

If you've already got a research question (or several) in mind, you're ahead of the game. If you're unsure where to get started, what would work for your project, or your questions are hopelessly vague, take heart, because you're not alone. Most archaeological practitioners have been in that very same spot, poised to go forth and do research without a clear question in mind.

Fortunately, there are numerous places to look for ideas, direction, and even fully formed research questions. Keep in mind that a research question doesn't usually have an expiration date. One of the most successful ways we push forward our knowledge of the archaeological record is by examining, reexamining, and breaking apart common questions that have not been satisfactorily answered. Already-asked questions are all around you, waiting to be gleaned for your project.

An obvious place to start in most circumstances is in published regional research designs and research syntheses. If you are willing to dig, you can also find great questions posed in reports on previous research efforts, often hidden amid the dull technical writing that distinguishes far too much CRM reporting. Your firm or institution may have a particular research focus that lends itself to your current work. Although we don't like to admit it, some (too many) research questions are the result of the academic fad of the moment. But for most of us, the most interesting, fun, and useful questions are the ones that you pose anew for yourself based on your foundation, regional knowledge, and personal research interests. These are the questions you'll care the most about and the ones that define the work that will give you the most satisfaction.

SOURCES OF QUESTIONS

The following aren't the only sources for research questions, but if you're at a loss as to where to begin, start with these leads.

- *Regional research designs.* One generally positive consequence of the sustained growth of CRM research is the existence of documents that synthesize what is known about the archaeology of a given region or topic and spell out research questions. These documents are variously termed *syntheses, overviews, regional research designs,* or *state* or *regional plans.* In many states, the SHPO has produced or commissioned such studies as part of its federal mandate. Other studies have been produced by or for federal agencies such as the Corps of Engineers (COE) and the Bureau of Land Management (BLM) or state agencies such as your Department of Transportation. Still other syntheses at the state and regional levels have been written by academic archaeologists on their own dime for their own reasons. In active regions, there may be many such sources of background knowledge and research questions. To find out what (if anything) exists in the area where you'll be working, the place to start is with the SHPO's office. The staff there will be aware of most of the syntheses and regional plans written for your state.

In addition to the SHPO, check also with any land-holding federal agencies that sponsor work in your area, such as the U.S. Army Corps of Engineers (COE), Bureau of Land Management (BLM), Forest Service, or National Park Service (NPS). They may have regional research designs which cross-cut state boundaries that the SHPO doesn't deal with regularly.

Lastly, don't forget your peer network. A quick phone call or e-mail to a few of your cohorts can lead you to obscure, newly published, or soon-to-be published syntheses or research designs that might fit the bill. Be forewarned that such documents can become outdated rather quickly in active research areas. You also need to find out whether the SHPO uses the syntheses and regional plans that might be in place. If the SHPO doesn't accept a regional research plan, using it as the foundation of your research effort could complicate your life.

- *Institutional focus.* Many archaeological organizations develop their own research focus. This can be a region, a time period, an archaeological culture, or a particular analytical or theoretical approach (see sidebar 5.1). If your institution has one or several such specialties, these should help you develop good research questions by building on what has already been done (e.g., filling in gaps or testing existing hypotheses). Often such institutional foci help strengthen your research proposals because the track record is already there. It is easier to sell your research ideas when your team includes experienced analysts who have a proven ability and the needed research tools such as comparative collections and specialized equipment. Don't panic if your organization has no research focus, but do keep in mind that experience and established expertise count a great deal.
- *Personal research interests.* Yes, you'd better have your own research interests. If you wake up one day after years of archaeological employment and find yourself without any particular research interests, it's past time for you to start considering an-

5.1. CENTER FOR ECOLOGICAL ARCHAEOLOGY AND ITS INSTITUTIONAL FOCUS

The Center for Ecological Archaeology (CEA) at Texas A&M University was an example of an archaeological research organization with a strong institutional focus. As the name indicates, this university-based contracting organization took an ecological approach to archaeology. The CEA sought out CRM and grant-funded projects within its main research region (broadly, the southern and eastern parts of Texas) that played to its strengths. Among its staff archaeologists were specialists in geoarchaeology and paleobotany. CEA also worked on a consulting basis with leading experts in soils, geology, zooarchaeology, and other ecological fields.

In the early 1990s, a CEA project took place within the giant foundation trench that was being dug to anchor a dam intended to create a municipal water supply reservoir near San Antonio. CEA archaeologists sampled a series of hunter-gatherer occupations up to twelve meters below the modern floodplain surface. As huge earth-moving machines worked their way downward, the archaeologists cordoned off relatively small areas so they could safely and quickly examine layer after layer of thin occupational lenses often separated by flood deposits. Over several years, the CEA's multidisciplinary research team was able to reveal the interwoven climatic, environmental, and cultural relationships of a ten-thousand-year record of human ecology. Through this project and many smaller ones, the CEA developed a strong research focus, one that gave it a competitive edge because of its proven ability to develop and follow through on scientific-based questions linked to ecology.

other career. It is difficult to design effective research unless you have an abiding interest in the outcome of your work. One of the big reasons lots of CRM work sucks is because the work is done only as a technical service instead of as a research effort. Most serious archaeologists develop many different research interests as their career progresses. Often these are unanticipated outgrowths of research opportunities. For example, one of us (Black) has become a minor expert on earth ovens after working at many sites where such features are common. This personal research interest has led to a number of projects where earth/rock ovens have been a central focus, as well as a series of workshops, presentations, and publications focused on experimental approaches to understanding earth ovens and other hot-rock cooking techniques. This focus has helped define highly targeted research questions regarding technology, subsistence, and site structure that continue to inform ongoing research projects. Such personal research interests are great sources of research questions because you are posing genuine problems from the strength of your prior experience and knowledge. Sustained interest in a topic helps you ask increasingly more productive questions.

- *Fads.* Fads play a big role in archaeological research, sometimes to the good, often not. Archaeological fads often begin when some big-name researcher publishes an article or book that attracts attention. If Lew Binford wrote an article about polyendemic resource procurement, the phrase (and the acronym PRP) would soon find its way into research proposals across the country, first in academia and then in CRM, regardless of whether it made any sense. Too often people latch onto buzzwords and leap on the latest intellectual bandwagon but neglect the real work that is required of substantive research. We've all seen new fads flash on the scene, make the quoting circles, and then fade away.

  The reason fads are fads, though, is that people are interested in them, and that interest does count in the world of CRM archaeology as it does in academia. The interest cuts two ways. One reason that fads fade so quickly is that while the white hot heat is on, lots of researchers are focused squarely on the target. Very quickly papers and reports start popping up that document every wart and pimple revealed by the emperor's new clothes. If you decide to go with a fad, make sure you follow it closely enough to keep current. Nothing is quite as foolish as putting all your research eggs in a faded basket whose bottom was ripped out by a lead article in *American Antiquity* two years ago.

- *Informed knowledge.* Perhaps the best source of research questions is an informed knowledge of what is known, what is worth knowing, and what is knowable in a given circumstance. This goes right back to your training and basic background knowledge as well as your career-long need to keep current. If you are well informed about the state of archaeological knowledge in the geographic and topical areas of interest, you'll see the gaps, holes, and questions worth pursuing in order to advance our understanding of the archaeological record. It starts with your background and builds with your current, up-to-date understanding of the regional record and the wider field of anthropological archaeology. When you throw in your personal and institutional research interests, you can't help but find interesting, exciting, fun research questions around which to focus your work.

Developing research questions is where you get the chance to exercise your archaeological imagination to best effect. The kinds of questions you pose at the beginning of the project will determine to a great extent how many of your colleagues will actually read your final report, how much interest will be generated in your work, and how many beers you will be fed to explain what you did and why. But if all we had to do was think up neat questions, we'd all be selling insurance by now. A good research question is only halfway there—to make a contribution, you need to have a shot at formulating an answer. You need questions for which you can reasonably expect to collect relevant data. So, as soon as you pose what you think is a good research question, you need to evaluate it before you commit yourself to action.

THINK THROUGH YOUR RESEARCH QUESTION— EXCAVATE IN YOUR MIND'S EYE

The value of your research question is relative to its cost and probability of success. Once you have a question in mind, simple or complex, you need to measure it against these acid tests:

- *What data do I need to address this question?* No cheating here. You need to think about this explicitly from an informed perspective. If your question is focused on seasonal resource scheduling, it's not enough to say, "I need preserved plant materials." You need the right kinds of plant materials from the right contexts. You will need data on associated artifacts and features, not to mention reliable dating to provide the cultural and chronological contexts that give meaning to all archaeological research questions. Think about all the data you're going to need. Then ask:
- *Is it likely that data needed to address this question can be obtained?* A useful research question in your region might be, "Were domesticated plants introduced in Late Archaic times, prior to heavy reliance on agriculture?" However, the reality may be that owing to the prevailing preservation conditions at the sites under investigation, you probably won't encounter the materials you need to address that question unless you see a way to infer incipient agriculture from the range of artifacts and features that you will actually encounter. Such indirect evidence may not provide an adequate basis to resolve your research question. So the first cut is

whether you, in your best archaeological judgment, believe that your field efforts will likely encounter the kinds of materials and contexts that will produce the data you need to attack your question. If you are confident that the data will be there to be gleaned, you must then ask:

- *Can I collect the data I need under the proposed scope of work?* Questions focused on materials recovered from deeply buried sites won't be of much use for a reconnaissance survey or limited testing program. At an equally practical level, your project budget may not cover the personnel to process and analyze flotation samples for large volumes of dirt or to cover a survey area at the level of resolution you'd need to produce data relevant to your questions. Logistics— time, place, money—control what you do and how you do it, to a large extent. The most elegant research question targeted at exactly the needed (and existing) data is not worth squat if you can't make the logistics work. Your questions need to point at data that you will be able to effectively collect and analyze within your project constraints. This leads to the final test:

- *Can I analyze and report the data in ways that effectively address the question?* It's not enough just to have the data in hand: You must have a workable plan to analyze and report the data so that it informs your research question. The old adage that you can figure out what it means back in the lab is a vestige of archaeology's heritage as a long-term academic endeavor. Tenured professors may have the luxury of taking their sweet time and of hauling lots of stuff back to the university without any concrete plan for completing the analysis. In the CRM world, a wealth of rich data doesn't help you much if you lack the skills, budget, or time to analyze and report it.

To take a personal example, when we excavated the Higgins site, an Archaic hunter-gatherer campsite, we used then state-of-the-art total data stations (TDSs) and collected incredible three-dimensional provenience data on more than thirty thousand artifacts. It was, and is, an awesome data set, rich with possibility. But because we didn't have the foresight to carefully consider how we would analyze and report this data, it was eventually collapsed into ten-centimeter-thick analytical units for comparison and analysis. It was cool, but it did not go very far toward addressing most of our research questions. We had not budgeted enough time to figure how to derive the data we'd hoped to use to deduce the subtle vertical patterning within the site. This experience highlights what is one of the most critical tests: All the sites, all the data in the world don't advance research much if it's beyond your capabilities to analyze and report them effectively.

Look at each one of your research questions with these tests in mind. A thorough job of thinking through your research questions will save you heartache, time, and money down the road. Once again, keep in mind that the process of thinking through your research questions is ongoing as the project unfolds. As new information, new constraints, and new opportunities become known, you will often need to rethink your initial research questions and run through the acid tests again. You may well find that your once-promising research question must bite the dust. Fine, but do yourself a favor and take a few minutes and write down a succinct and honest justification for why you abandoned your research question. The same goes if you have come up with a new question—think it through and write it down.

Armed with a thorough scope of work and a good set of research questions, you are ready to focus a little closer and figure out how these problems can be incorporated within a workable strategy or research plan.

6

DEVELOPING YOUR RESEARCH STRATEGY

Your research design is part of a larger strategy, a strategy that joins the work you have to do, the resources you have at your disposal, and the research you hope to accomplish. To be effective, this strategy needs to be two-pronged: archaeological and operational. Your archaeological strategy addresses the data collection, sampling, and analytical methods you plan to use to accomplish your research goals. Just as important (and often ignored), your operational strategy needs to address the logistical, organizational, and political needs of your project.

THINK FIRST, DIG LATER— ARCHAEOLOGICAL STRATEGY

Developing a successful archaeological strategy is hard, so you have to *think before you dig*. The larger and more complex the research project, the more thinking ahead you must do. Your job is to clearly understand what it is you are trying to accomplish, within all the contexts you're working in—the natural and cultural landscapes, the regulations, and the sponsor's time constraints. While the concept of thinking before you dig sounds obvious, archaeologists are notorious for arriving in the field without much of a game plan. Oh, sure, the typical archaeological project today follows some sort of research design, but far too often the research strategy boils down to little more than "Let's dig some holes and hope we find something interesting"—archaeology by default.

The mind-set that there is a limited and proven set of correct or standard ways to do things relieves the archaeologist from the responsibility of thinking. Making strategic decisions means explicitly examining the standards and alternatives and stating explicitly from the outset what you will be doing. For others to judge the work you do, the data you collect, and the conclusions you reach, they need to understand how you did the work. Your strategy is the way you define the work you'll do, for yourself and your peers.

Several important elements comprise your archaeological strategy. First you need to focus on the data you need or hope to collect to address your research questions. If your questions have to do with seasonality, you may want to collect floral or faunal data. What kind of materials will you target to get the data you need? Linked inexorably to the data are the methods you'll use to collect your materials and make your observations. If you are targeting plant remains, will you use flotation to collect the light fraction for sorting? Do you need to use a chemical process to break the bonds of a heavy clay soil? How will that affect delicate plant materials and the suitability of surviving plant remains for radiocarbon dating? A big part of any archaeological strategy must address your approach to sampling. Will your float samples be taken from features only? How will that affect the analysis? What size constant-volume sample would provide a reliable background sample? You need to look at how you'll manage your data in the field and how materials will be processed back in the lab. If you're using a total data station (TDS) to collect provenience records, do you have a system in place to ensure against bad shots? Do you have lab procedures in place so that all your samples will be processed in a standard manner? And last, consider how you'll ultimately analyze the data. Will you be trying to compare relative frequencies of materials across or between sites? If so, how will you ensure that the sample sizes are equivalent?

These elements of your archaeological strategy are interdependent and causally linked. Remember, your job isn't to find the perfect strategy but rather to settle on one that will work and, most critically, to make your strategy explicit. Spell out what you're going to do and how you're going to do it. When you've done this, you've made a contribution to the archaeological record, regardless of what you find in the field. By presenting an explicit research strategy, you're providing the archaeological community with a record of what worked and what didn't, and probably some good insights into why. This is the information we all need if we're going to learn and move our field forward.

DEFINING YOUR DATA

First things first: The first thing you need to do is explicitly define the data you want to collect to address your research questions. But what do we mean by data? Data aren't stuff, not dart points, not rim sherds, not even a nice postmold. *Data are systematic observations.* Data may be a properly completed unit level record form, a provenience record for an artifact, or a field interpretation of an artifact type. No data exist until an observation is recorded. The distinction between things and data is basic and critical. The problem is that when we think about things as data, it's all too easy (and common) to point to a pile of things and say, "There's X, Y, Z; anyone can see that," when, in fact, hardly anyone else will see that pile of things the same way that you do. When we recognize that data are observations, we have to be more explicit. "We can tell this is X, because we can see Y and Z." When we're explicit in the way we define our data, the data we collect are more reliable and easier to analyze. And it's only when we're explicit that our peers can make the best use of our data, our work, and our analysis.

One of the first questions you need to ask yourself when you focus on the data for your project is "What is the useful level of resolution for each class of data?" You may want to map the density of artifacts within the excavated areas to identify functional components of a site. If you excavate by ten-centimeter levels on a 1×1–meter grid and collect artifacts from the screen, the level of resolution for your map will be one meter horizontally and ten centimeters vertically. If the patterns you're looking for are larger than $1 \times 1 \times 0.1$ meter, then you're probably in good shape. If the patterns are smaller than that, your data are ill suited for this type of analysis. Focusing on the different data sets you hope to collect and defining them explicitly will help remove needless ambiguities from your archaeological strategy.

DATA AND METHODS

It's easy to see how data and methods are linked in a causal chain that follows right through to your analysis. Your methods define and limit the data you can collect. For instance, if you screen the soil from your site through quarter-inch mesh, you'll find it difficult to develop a reliable microdebitage data set. Not only do your methods constrain your data, but the data you collect also set limits on the type and character of the analyses you can perform. What you learn from your work is a direct product of the methodological choices you make right at the beginning.

As you look at a set of data, you should be focusing as well on the methods you'll use to collect it. Define your methods explicitly. If you want to collect constant-volume samples to develop a data set on microdebitage distribution, where are you going to collect them, how are you going to collect them, and what size will they be? How will their locations be measured? Is the depth measured from the top? Bottom? How will their locations be recorded? How will the samples be processed? How will the fractions be analyzed? How will the data from the fraction analysis be matched up with the field observations? It's not as simple as "Take one hundred cubic centimeters of soil, and count the flakes." Every decision you make on the methods you'll use to collect your data will—not *might*, not *could*—will affect the data you collect.

Archaeological field methods are the subject of many books and college courses as well as several of the other volumes of The Archaeologist's Toolkit. Wherever you work in archaeology, you will quickly learn the preferred and expected field methods. Often you will get the distinct impression that there is only one right way to do a given task. Nothing exemplifies this like the square hole—the one-meter square that is the basic provenience unit for so much archaeological work. While there are many reasons why square holes make good sense in many different circumstances, there is a wide world of archaeology beyond the square hole.

Methods should be chosen to fit the logistical circumstances and *to yield the targeted data*, not strictly because of expectation or habit—not archaeology by default. The standard, default methods may well be appropriate for your project. They provide consistency and comparability when properly executed. But even if you choose to rest your butt in the well-worn comfort of the "usual" methods, you need to spell out exactly what that means. Just as people have different perceptions of data, "standard" methods seldom are. The small differences—where the depth of a level is measured, what is collected from the screen, the acceptable error in elevation shots—can loom large when data sets are compared.

By carefully defining your methods (and your data), you're building the framework to ensure that the observations that make up your data are being made consistently. This helps you and the people collecting your data. It helps others understand what the data you collect represent. And it provides the background that other researchers need to evaluate your analysis and write-up. Your ultimate goal isn't to create data sets that you alone can analyze and publish. Your goal is to add to our knowledge of the archaeological record. To do that, you need to work to create *reliable* data sets that other researchers can use. The only way to make your data reliable (just like it says—so others can count on it) is to document the data and the methods you used to collect them.

SAMPLING STRATEGIES

Tangled up in data and methods is sampling. We won't go into formal sampling methods here, as statistical methods are beyond the scope of this book. Our favorite published discussion of sampling strategy in archaeology is Kent Flannery's book *The Early Mesoamerican Village* (1976). This humorous yet serious account highlights theoretical and practical aspects of sampling on regional and site levels. You will also find discussions of sampling strategies in the other Archaeologist's Toolkit volumes.

Beyond formal sampling techniques, you should recognize that all archaeological research uses sampling strategies. It is impossible to completely survey, excavate, or study the entire universe. When we collect materials to study or make observations to add to our research data, we are making sampling decisions. When you decide what survey interval to use in a pedestrian survey or reconnaissance, you're making an explicit sampling decision. Your research strategy needs to address explicitly whether this sample will yield the data you need to address your question. If it can, then it's a good strategy. Sampling strategies are part and parcel of the methods you'll use to collect your data.

One of the aspects of sampling that we often ignore is what to do with materials that won't provide data to illuminate the stated research problems. Do you collect all those snail shells on the screen even though you need only a few? Archaeologists have the bad habit of trying to collect everything just because it is there and might someday be useful to someone for something. Materials collected fortuitously and off-hand observations can provide interesting sidelights to your research and can sometimes provide valuable avenues of analysis in and of themselves. But because of tight budgets and strained resources, we also have to consider the costs—in time, money, and space—to process and curate those materials. Like most knotty problems, there is no easy answer; it's something we have to deal with on a case-by-case basis. You should develop an effective sampling strategy that focuses on the data you know you need and preserves enough samples of the rest of the encountered material record so that other kinds of problems can be investigated later.

LAB PROCESSING AND DATA MANAGEMENT

It's easy to ignore the lab processing and data management aspects of your work until the day your bags of materials are stacked on the lab shelf. But the methods you use to collect your data don't stop at the lab door. You should be just as explicit in defining how the materials from the field will be processed and analyzed as you would be in defining how to take a soil sample. Lab folks often are better organized than their field counterparts, so if you have a regular lab staff, they probably already have a set of documentation outlining their standard procedures. The goal, again, is to produce a reliable data set. When you're knee deep in the analysis, you (and anyone else who hopes to use it) must know how the data you're using were generated. The recipe is simple: Explicitly define how your materials will be processed and how your observations will be made.

The data, the observations that are taken in the field and the lab, must be organized and accessible if you are going to use them effectively. Data management is at the core of effectively analyzing your expensive and explicit data. When we think of data management, we usually think of computer databases. But data management isn't just computers. Data management means organizing your data so that they are accessible and safe. Photocopying pages from your field notebook every week and storing them in a binder in the lab is a good way to protect that data from loss—and it's data management. Field forms stuffed into an artifact box with muddy soil samples won't yield the best-quality data, and your data management plan has an obvious hole. Your strategy needs to include how you will move data from the field to the lab to analysis—all the data. You need to plan for problems and develop data management strategies to avoid data loss (e.g., if it's raining, put the field forms in a plastic zip-top bag).

There probably aren't many archaeological projects on the planet today where computers aren't being used. But remember, there is a price to pay. Computers don't really make anything easier, simpler, or less expensive. They require capital investment, power, training, and support. What computers can do is allow us to work with larger and more complex data sets, to do more complex work. But they don't do it by themselves. If your strategy is to use computers to help manage your data, you need to pay the price up front. You need to consider your data, your methods, your sampling strategies, your lab processing, and your analytical needs when putting together your database. You need to ask and answer questions like these: Will data be input in the lab? In the field? Both? How will data be merged? How will data entry be verified?

How can data be reused (for artifact tags, accession cards, etc.)? And the big one: How will we want to retrieve these data during the analysis? Having a well-considered (and, again, documented) data management strategy is a key part of ensuring that the data you need will be there when you need them.

ANTICIPATING THE ANALYSIS

Once you've considered your data and planned your methodological attack, you need to take it a step farther. How will you analyze these data to inform you on your research questions? It's all too easy (and common) to run out to the field, grub up a bunch of stuff, take a pile of field notes, and say to ourselves, "We'll figure it out in the lab." Well, if the data don't match up with the questions you're trying to ask, or if you can't retrieve the data you need, you're screwed, plain and simple. The entire process of developing an archaeological strategy is recursive—you look from your data back to your questions, and from your methods to your data, and from your sampling strategies to your methods, and finally you should consider how your analysis will illuminate your research questions. And from there you look back again at your data, methods, and sampling.

As with the rest of your archaeological strategy, you need to be explicit in defining your analysis. Recognize from the outset that your approach may change, but consider how you would proceed today if you had the data you plan to recover in hand. Just as defining your methods will help you maintain control in data collection, documenting how you plan to analyze the data can provide a jump start to that part of the work and helps keep the focus on the research questions at hand.

FINAL STEPS

The last step in planning your archaeological strategy is to critically review your questions, data, methodology, and analysis. Get someone else—preferably an experienced critical thinker—to read it over and critique it (better now than when it's too late). Where are the holes? What are the hang-ups? You may need to reconsider parts of your questions, which will change aspects of your data and analysis. Stepping through this recursive process in the planning stage pays benefits throughout the course of your research.

Everything costs, in time, money, and energy. Every archaeological research project has limits. You can't make informed, strategic decisions unless and until you take a hard-nosed look at the costs and benefits of each component of your developing research design. Thinking first also means weighing the costs versus the benefits of everything you do.

MAKING TOUGH CHOICES—OPERATIONAL STRATEGY

In the CRM world, you have to make tough choices to balance your research needs against the pressures of time, money, logistics, politics, and bureaucracy. Too often archaeologists are unwilling or unable to make the tough decisions that must be made when, as always, budgets aren't big enough and field seasons aren't quite long enough to do everything we'd like. Without careful planning, these pressures can wedge you into a "dig and figure" mode: You dig stuff up and hope to figure it out later.

As you develop your research strategy, real-world considerations should loom large. Like it or not, you're operating within bureaucratic, logistical, and financial contexts that control what you do and when you do it. A common approach to these complications is to pretend that they don't exist and rail against them when they insistently worm their way into your daily routine. It can be satisfying to ignore repeated calls from your sponsor's accounting department—until the bills come due, and no check is forthcoming. Dodging calls from that regulator about an overdue report makes good bar talk until they put the kibosh on your permit for that new job. You've also got a budget, and a schedule, and people not showing up for work, and broken-down trucks all to make your life a lot more interesting than you'd really like. Getting a handle on all of these things is the other half of your research strategy—it's your strategy for getting things done, your operational strategy.

WORKING WITH BUREAUCRACIES

As a CRM archaeologist, you often have the joy of working with one, or two, or even three or more unique and interesting bureaucracies. You'll almost certainly be dealing with your SHPO reviewers and regulators. If your sponsor is a government agency, you'll have to deal with it and its environmental folks. Whether your organization is large or small, you also have your own bureaucracy to deal with. When we talk about bureaucracy, we're talking about people, people who are trying—for the most part, trying their best—to implement the policies of their organizations. A lot of times, inane bureaucratic BS seems just as inane to the folks who are wielding the bureaucratic stick.

There's one very simple strategy for working with organizations: just deal with them as people (see sidebar 6.1). Find out who you'll be dealing with at each organization. If you don't know them, give them a phone call, introduce yourself, and explain what you'll be working on. If at all possible, arrange to come by and meet them in person. There's no big agenda, just a quick hello and a reminder about the project you'll both be involved in. When you can put human faces to a faceless organization, it will make dealing with bureaucracies much more pleasant. Conversely, the bureaucrats will see you, too, as a person, rather than as an anonymous cog in another annoying project wheel.

PERMITS

Another aspect of working with bureaucracies is dealing with permits. Most government-mandated research requires some sort of permit from a state, federal, or tribal authority. Permits may have very specific, legally binding requirements that can greatly impact your research project. These requirements range from prescribed qualifications for the permit holder to the type of work allowed, the area where the work will be performed, and the time frame within which the work must be completed. As soon as the project is contracted, contact your SHPO and any other agencies involved to get moving on the permits.

In some cases, you may be working under the aegis of an agency's permit or memorandum of agreement (MOA). Some federal agencies such as the Corps of Engineers (COE) negotiate MOAs and programmatic agreements with SHPOs to cover the routine archaeological work they anticipate doing on the properties they manage. In those cases, you're relieved of the responsibility for permitting the project yourself.

In many cases, though, you will be responsible for getting the project permitted and ensuring that the terms of the permit are met. Once you know the project area, your SHPO office can tell you what the permit requirements will be for the project. This is serious business. Permits are generally issued to an individual, and if your project

6.1. KEEPING THE PEACE: PEOPLE IN YOUR OPERATIONAL STRATEGY

It's important to have a strategy for dealing with all of the players in the CRM field. Each of these folks has an interest in your work, and keeping them happy—or at least quiescent—can make the difference between living in harmony and living hell.

Sponsors

Naturally, you will need to plan for interaction with the folks who are sponsoring your research and handing out the bucks. They may have no real interest in the work, or they may find it fascinating and want to be closely involved. A healthy professional relationship is your best strategy. Keep your sponsors happy by keeping them informed and by understanding and doing your best to accommodate their schedules and concerns while maintaining your credibility as an ethical archaeologist. Boot-licking client servers are respected by no one. It's much better to earn their respect by doing your job well and paying attention to the details that matter to them.

Regulators

You ignore your regulators at your own peril. How you maintain lines of communication depends on the context of your particular project. It could be as simple as making a phone call once a month or as complex as submitting detailed progress reports. The most consistently successful strategy is to develop a healthy professional relationship with your regulators based on mutual respect and cooperation. An antagonistic relationship is always counterproductive and not very bright on your part.

fails to fulfill the requirements of the permit, it is your professional life that is on the line. Read and understand the requirements of the permit, and if you have any questions at all, be sure to ask before it's too late.

As your project progresses, stay in touch with the folks who issued your permit. If you see that you won't be able to make a required deadline, contact the permitting office as soon possible. If you make the effort to be honest and forthright with your permitting agencies, you can avoid a lot of needless hassle. Remember, though, rules are rules and being honest and up-front won't necessarily cut you any slack if you've really screwed up. Most permitting agencies try to be even-handed, and part of that is doling out the bad with the good. That's why you need to take permits seriously.

Research Team

Building a cohesive and effective research team requires more than keeping each team member informed about his or her particular piece of the action. Make sure all the members of your team know the big picture and have a chance to follow the project as it unfolds. Give the lab staff a chance to visit and take part in the fieldwork so they will gain a much better appreciation of the material they are processing. Specialized analysts do a better job when they know the overall objectives of the research and when they develop a good feel for the site and its environs. It's up to you to plot a strategy that creates a successful team.

Peers

Your fellow archaeologists have a legitimate stake in your work because we share common professional goals and depend on one another for information. Therefore, part of your strategy should be to keep your peers informed through conference presentations, progress reports, well-written and accessible final reports, and peer-reviewed journal articles. When possible, invite your archaeological colleagues to visit your field project—show them what you're doing and ask for their observations.

The Public

This is the most difficult operational arena for many archaeologists because we are not trained in communicating and marketing our work to a wide audience. Increasingly, however, archaeologists are learning to develop innovative strategies for involving and engaging the public (see Toolkit, volume 7). Through open houses, volunteer programs, public displays, TV shows, educational videos, websites, public lectures, media events, and popular accounts, archaeologists must ensure our own survival by making our work relevant to those who we ultimately serve.

LOGISTICS

This is where the rubber meets the road, the nuts and bolts of getting people to the field, getting data to the lab, making sure everybody gets paid on time and the outhouse is limed. As you plot your research strategy, you need to look sharply at the time lines, budget, and staff and use your experience and judgment to see whether you can actually do all the work you've planned. Don't forget to figure in weather days, mechanical breakdown, crew loss, and administrative blowouts. Your scope of work outlines what must be done; here you need to really focus on what *can* be done. If you don't feel that you've got the experience you need to make these judgments, call on a colleague with more notches in her belt.

Staffing—having the right people at the right time—can make or break a project. If you're planning to staff the field crew with graduate or undergraduate students on summer break, your five-month field season is going to be problematic. It's more than just having enough bodies on hand. Most successful research projects are accomplished by well-matched teams of people with the right skills and the right attitude. This comes back to the importance of thinking and planning ahead. You have to put together your budget long before you start hiring people. If you have tried to cut costs by planning to pay cheap wages, you will probably end up with an inexperienced crew or one made up of disgruntled, low-achiever types no one else will hire. This is especially true when the CRM economy is in full swing and jobs are plentiful. Supply and demand.

The best way to make sure that you've crossed your logistical *t*'s is to use a checklist. Setting up a checklist of what you need and when you need it is also a good way to focus on equipment, personnel, and supplies while you're writing a proposal or a budget (see appendix D, "The Logistics Checklist"). Using a good checklist is an easy way to help ensure that you've got what you need when you need it. Logistics is more than staffing and supplies, though. Your strategy has to include the administrative end of the logistics train. You need to have a plan for making sure that the paychecks come on time and that per diem is there when the crew is hungry. It may be as simple as wrangling some help from the office administrative assistant, or it may mean creating another checklist of things you need to do at the end of each week. Putting an effective strategy in place boils down to defining what the tasks are (write it down!) and making sure that everyone knows what needs to be done.

Logistics isn't fun and it doesn't seem like archaeology, but working out the how, when, and where is essential to the success of any research project. The graveyard of wrecked archaeological careers is littered with the corpses of the logistically impaired.

THE BUDGET

The budget is an evil, immutable, unyielding force grinding slowly and painfully over your grand plans. Once you've set a budget, you need to develop a strategy for executing your research within it. It's critical to develop a realistic budget up front. But even the most finely crafted budget can fall victim to unexpected problems, crew disasters, and rising prices. This is where the decisions get hard.

The first thing you should do with your budget is to place your analysis and write-up money off limits. When you're in the field, there will be all kinds of unexpected expenses, and it will be tempting to say, "We're not finding any charcoal, so we won't really need those extra five carbon dates." But there are unexpected expenses in the lab, analysis, and write-up as well. Don't touch that money until its time comes.

Next, list all the things you can jettison in each phase of the project if money gets tight. The strategy here is to plan for a kind of financial triage, to choose the parts of your work that you can allow to die so that the project can live. As you do this, you need to balance your research needs against their costs in real dollars. If your research questions are focused on seasonality, you probably can't afford to eliminate your botanical analyst. But you may be able to forego excavation of additional units where the soils don't seem to support the kind of preservation you're interested in.

Last, if the budget is impossibly tight or you have a major disaster, contact your SHPO and your sponsor immediately. We can't emphasize enough the value of close communication. Everyone is truly interested in getting the work completed. Calling your sponsor to report that you're going to run out of time before the work is finished won't be fun, but it can head off total disaster. Going to the sponsor or the SHPO to report that you're out of money shouldn't be a deceitful ploy to get more funding. It's critical that you be completely honest and aboveboard. In a recent case in our area, a contractor found that its crew would not be able to complete its work within the existing budget (which, stupidly, covered only the fieldwork). The sponsor refused to provide any more funds, so the contractor simply walked away from the site, leaving half-completed excavation units open and unprotected. This was a disaster for everyone involved, most of all for the archaeology. When you see a budget problem on the horizon, you need to have a strategy to deal with it rationally, to fulfill your obligation to the sponsor and, most of all, to the archaeological record.

THE SCHEDULE

No matter how much money you have, no matter the skill of the crew, the length of the day, or the speed of your trowel, you will not have enough time to do all the things you want to do. Your time is constrained by the budget, but you'll also have other pressures eating away at the time you have. If you have a crew of students, the opening day of classes will likely see a sharp drop-off in production. If you work in the Southwest or the Great White North (somewhere up past Oklahoma, we hear), the high heat of summer or the icy blasts of winter can limit your days in the field. Or it could be monsoons, or black flies, or a construction schedule—whatever it is, time is immutable.

You need to manage your time just like your budget. Your schedule should allow for weather delays and other problems. Look at your schedule and anticipate problems. Prioritize your work with regard to time as well as money, and be ready with the phone numbers of your sponsor and the SHPO. Your goal is to balance your research needs against the time you have available to do the work. Again, communication is the key. If you see a problem looming, talk it over with all the folks involved. There may be solutions you haven't yet seen.

Your time strategy, like your budget strategy, is to maintain the greatest measure of control you can in the face of unanticipated problems. You can't anticipate everything, but you can be ready for problems by focusing now on the tough choices you may need to make later and hammering out a realistic schedule.

INVOLVING THE PUBLIC

An often overlooked aspect of most CRM work is planning to involve the public. Since they pay the bills and generally support the laws that sponsor most of our research, we need to spend some energy and time of our own to acknowledge and encourage their interest. Some large CRM projects have public information aspects built in by the sponsor—maybe an informational brochure will be produced or a museum exhibit will be developed. More likely there is no plan nor a budget to engage the public in the work you're doing.

Sad fact first: Most of us archaeologists can't write our way out of a paper bag. Years of churning out CRM reports have imbued most of us with the writing style of a stale bagel. Your strategy for sharing information about the work you're doing and getting the public engaged in your work should involve working with people who can and do write for public consumption. Sometimes a project sponsor requires production of a brochure or other popular treatment that they plan to distribute to the public. Often these materials are written in turgid, dumbed-down archaeo-jargon and please nobody, so they languish in boxes somewhere and don't accomplish the worthy goal of giving something back to the public. The archaeologists aren't happy, and the sponsors aren't happy. The intention is good, though, so when presented with the opportunity to prepare a popular product, swallow your pride and farm the job out. Find someone who has experience reaching a general audience, a journalist who writes for the audience you intend to reach, a writer with credits in periodicals that reach your audience, a videographer with experience in documentaries. These things aren't cheap, so if your sponsor wants to tack on $500 to produce a "quick brochure," tactfully decline. Neither of you will be happy with the result.

You don't have to be James Michener or Brian Fagan, though, to reach a general audience with good, solid information about your archaeological project. People in the communities where you're working are interested in what you're doing there. With no more complex skills than being able to answer questions about your work intelligently, you can get the good word out about what archaeologists do and the value of the archaeological record.

Before you embark on any plans for including the public, be sure you run them past your sponsor. Some sponsors will jump at the chance to look good, but some have deeply ingrained institutional paranoia. Work with those you can.

The first step is to find out whether your sponsor or client has a public relations or communications department responsible for generating good press. If they do, contact them and give them the scoop on your planned work. You can help them write a short press release that they'll send to all the newspapers, radio stations, and TV stations in the area where you'll be working. A local angle is gold for these folks, so you might even be contacted by reporters for interviews, photos, or maybe a live radio spot.

If your sponsor doesn't have a PR department, you can do it yourself. Write a one-page summary of the work you're doing that explains why it is interesting and important. Keep it simple. Include information about scheduling and how to contact your project. Send copies to the local papers, radio stations, and TV stations. If even one small-town paper runs a piece on your project, more people probably will read that article than your final report—a depressing thought but one that should spur you to action.

Another way to reach the public is through presentations to community groups. Giving presentations is a great way to focus your ideas about the work you do, and the more presentations you give, the easier—and more fun—it gets. If you're going to be in the field for a month or two, contact local community organizations like the

Optimists or Lions Club. They are always looking for people to give thirty-minute presentations at their monthly meetings, and a live archaeologist is quite a catch. Talk about both the local area and the big picture, adding the human element as much as possible—those are the things the audience will find most interesting.

Another excellent and fun way to include the public is with an open house. Try to schedule it on a weekend so as many people as possible can attend, and use the local media, schools, and community organizations to get the word out. Plan for a crowd, and do your best to have your crew working—people love to see archaeologists actually doing things rather than just pointing at square holes and jawing. People are fascinated with archaeology, and the opportunity to see what it's like in action will almost always draw a crowd. A few years ago in New Mexico we drew many more than four hundred people one cold, drizzly Saturday morning to look at some open units, see the flakes and pot sherds that had been collected, and ask questions about what we were doing. Volume 7 in the Toolkit series has even more information.

CONCLUSION

Your research strategy is the sum of two parts: the archaeological strategy and the operational strategy. You need both to make the most of your opportunity to engage in archaeological research. It may be that you write out parts of your strategy, or you might just think through them and get a game plan straight in your head. It's a matter of degree—a small three-day survey doesn't demand the same level of planning that a six-month excavation does. However you conceptualize your research strategy, if you work through the elements discussed here, you've got your research design right at hand.

THE WRITTEN RESEARCH DESIGN

Your written research design can take many forms—a revised scope of work, a proposal, a work plan, a formal research design, or part of a letter or a contract outlining what you have agreed to do. Usually it's part of the package you prepare for your sponsor to win a contract (or funding agency to win a grant). Occasionally it's a stand-alone document written later, after the contract is signed, to satisfy the funding, regulating, or permitting agencies. Whatever its form, most written research designs tend to focus on the problem orientation and the methodological aspects of research.

A good research design acknowledges the contexts of the work, addresses the concerns of the various players, spells out the scope of the work, outlines the approach to be taken, describes the research problems and the targeted data, and links these to appropriate field and analytical methods (see sidebar 7.1). When a research design is created solely to win a contract or grant, it's little more than a pretense—a slick pile of verbiage filed away and forgotten once the work begins. A well-done research design is a dynamic tool used by all the players involved to focus the field work, analysis, reporting, and evaluation of the project.

7.1. YOUR WRITTEN RESEARCH DESIGN CHECKLIST

1. Before you finalize your research design, show it to an experienced colleague and members of your research team, and ask for feedback. Sometimes the SHPO will agree to review your draft document. Getting feedback takes time, so plan ahead and don't put it off to the last minute.
2. Treat your research design just like any other professional document. Check the spelling, have it edited, make certain all the text references are matched by those in the "references cited," format it consistently, and use headings and subheadings to improve the organization.
3. Acid-test your plan by trying to reread it from the perspective of your audience. What do they expect? Look for BS, hyperbole, naïveté, and other common faults.
4. Don't confuse jargon for clear thinking or scholarship. Plain English is the way to go. Make it easy to read and follow.
5. When you think you are done, go back over your scope of work one last time, and make sure your research design responds appropriately.
6. Make certain that you credit other people's ideas, particularly those in print. Plagiarism and sloppy scholarship are sure signs of incompetence.
7. Avoid the dazzler approach of using fancy paper, special binders, and gratuitous color bar graphs. The sharp reader will recognize these ploys for what they are: smoke and mirrors intended to dress up a feeble document. Dazzle them instead with your coherent ideas and pragmatic attention to necessary detail.
8. Don't promise the sky—you cannot do it all. Focus, focus, focus, and make your research count by homing in on important but narrow problems that you can realistically address. Write a doable plan.

WHOM ARE YOU WRITING FOR?

As always, knowing your audience allows you to communicate more effectively. In the CRM world, five audiences may be reading and (hopefully) using your research design:

- *Clients or sponsors.* These are usually nonarchaeologists who are mainly interested in the time and cost aspects of your work.
- *Contract administrators and regulators.* These are archaeologists working for your sponsors and in the SHPO office. Their main interest is in making sure that the various state and federal laws (NHPA, ARPA, NAGPRA, etc.) are followed and that the archaeological work is up to snuff (a very relative term in the wide world of CRM archaeology).

- *The archaeologists and specialists who will be part of your team.* Your crew and consultants will use your research design to help understand their role and to focus what they do.
- *Your peers.* Other archaeologists in your area may be keenly interested in how your strategy and results can inform their own research, or they may just want to kibitz.
- *Most important, yourself.* The act of writing down what you plan to do is one of the most effective ways of focusing your thoughts. Things that seem obvious and simple when floating around in the thick gruel of your brain show all their warts and flaws when laid out in black and white. Writing your research design allows you to hone your ideas and your half-formed thoughts into a concrete and effective plan for wringing knowledge from the sparse and challenging archaeological record.

Keep these various audiences in mind as you write. Tell a sponsor that you are planning to "seek subsistence data on the Early Archaic," and he may shrug and assume that you know what you are doing. Tell a SHPO reviewer the same thing, and she might say, "What the heck do you mean? Don't you realize that Early Archaic sites in this region almost never have any preserved organic remains?" The archaeologically knowledgeable people who have control over your work will look at your research design to determine whether you are asking appropriate questions, proposing appropriate methods, seeking appropriate data, and planning a feasible chunk of work for the circumstance. If they are competent and doing their jobs, they will read your document with a critical eye. Knowing your readers allows you to do a better job of communicating your ideas in ways they will understand.

An all-too-often neglected use of a research design is to inform those who are on your research team about the game plan. If you have gone to the trouble of writing a research design, why not let your crew members and consultants read it as soon as they come on board? This is common sense—people who know the plan are in a much better position to be able to contribute. On one large survey project we survived, the field director told the crew that we were there only to serve as his "hands and eyes" and would be informed about the research strategy only "on a need-to-know basis." Bad for morale, bad for research. The most productive research projects are those in which the crew members and consultants are actively informed and work as an integrated team. By circulating your research design to those you work with, your crew members and consultants become research team members and colleagues working toward a common goal.

Your archaeological peers are likely to be your toughest critics and may well read your research design years after the fact. There is plenty of nit-picking criticism, petty bickering, and spiteful quarreling in archaeology. You can't avoid it; all you can do is try to minimize it by doing the best work possible. Part of that is learning to take criticism for what it's worth and to use it to make your work even better (see sidebar 7.2).

This takes us back to the most important audience—you. Your research design really isn't for SHPO Joe, or Sponsor Sue, or Professor Punwit down at the university. It's a tool you create to help you do your work. You're the one with the most to lose—or gain. A thorough and well-conceived research design will improve your chances of winning the contract, help you create a productive research atmosphere, and serve as your blueprint for success from start to finish.

7.2. MORE CRITICISM, PLEASE!

An essential and often unrecognized skill in archaeology is learning to deal with criticism. Most of us have an automatic, defensive reaction when we're criticized. But think for a moment about how rare it is to get feedback of any kind. Without feedback, the only guiding voice you have is the all-too-familiar sound of your own opinion.

Exchanging ideas and critiquing work is absolutely essential in a productive research environment. This is why all leading journals are peer reviewed. The review process in CRM sometimes involves agency review of draft reports. But when criticism happens only after the fact, there's usually not much you can do but shrug your shoulders. That's why it is so important to get feedback—criticism—early and throughout the research process. Good, focused criticism can help you concentrate on what you're doing and help find flaws or unrealized research potentials. It's not enough to graciously accept criticism; seek it out and use it as a whetstone to keep your research sharp.

Positive strokes are easy enough to accept, but harsh criticism often really hurts. If you let it, it can destroy your self-confidence, and no matter how self-assured you are, disapproving evaluations are upsetting. That's why you need a strategy to turn criticism to your own purposes:

1. Evaluate the critic's motives and abilities. Is he just a jerk with a personal grudge? Maybe she is just too ignorant to recognize the merit of your work (this one's always handy). But maybe the critics just don't know how to frame criticism in constructive terms. Don't lash back at critics, no matter how mean

PROJECTS BIG AND SMALL

When we're talking about archaeological projects and research designs, size does matter a great deal. So does purpose. A research design for a small project intended to answer basic compliance questions— "Are sites present?" and "Are they potentially significant?"—is a much different beast from a research design for a multiyear mitigation project or an ongoing academic research program. For small CRM projects, the formal document will probably be little more than a revised scope of work, coupled with a budget and a contract or a letter authorizing you to do the work. In contrast, the larger projects will almost certainly require much more thorough documentation and justification of your research plan. Despite such real-world differences, there is still a commonality here: An informed research perspective is equally critical to the success of projects big and small.

spirited or harsh they seem; it makes you feel good only for a minute. If the criticism is truly nasty, intended only to make the insecure critic feel superior, dismiss it—it's your critic's problem, not yours.

2. Mine the criticism for valid or useful points. The most stinging critiques usually identify something you missed or ignored. Make a list of the things you can use—actually write them down. There is always something you can use in every critique, even if it is just to avoid sending any more draft manuscripts to that jerk. As you work through the critique try to remember the critic's point of view. If she is a pottery expert and seems to harp continually over what you think are typological minutiae, she could simply be looking at it from her particular perspective—or else your pottery analysis really does stink.

3. Acknowledge the effort of the critics. They've taken the time to read or think about your work and have reacted to it, and you stand to benefit. Write a short note to the critics, thank them for their time, and offer yourself to review their work in the future. If the critique is part of a formal review process, note every comment and suggestion and respond to each one. If you can't accommodate a suggestion, tell the reviewer or sponsor why not.

4. Seek out criticism. Your best critics are often the colleagues and associates whose work you respect. Ask them to critique your work, formally or informally. It's easy: Just ask them what they think, and take what they give you to heart. None of us has a corner on the archaeology market, and the way we really learn is by exchanging our ideas. We really mean it when we say, "More criticism, please"!

Most small projects don't require elaborate justification, a detailed methodology, or a big research question, but they do require an informed research perspective and a clear understanding of what will be done. Big projects will always require a lot more in the way of a written research design. Many projects fall in between these extremes—they will require more than a simple scope of work and a letter and a less-than-sixty-page treatise. We can't tell you how much detail you will need. You have to decide based on your experience and the requirements of the particular research project you are designing. But no matter the size or scope of your research design, it should hit five key areas: (1) scope of work and legal rationale, (2) problem definition, (3) data definition, (4) methods and techniques, and (5) analysis.

CRITICAL COMPONENTS OF YOUR WRITTEN RESEARCH DESIGN

The components presented here are the basis for any well-developed research design. How you put them together, how extensive they are, and how the document itself is presented are simply variations on a theme. Your sponsor or SHPO may have a preferred form, so be sure you find that out before you start to write. Become a student of research designs—keep a file of research designs you've glommed onto from other projects, successful and unsuccessful. These can help you get a sense of what is expected in your area, but remember, this is your research design, so think for yourself.

SCOPE OF WORK AND LEGAL RATIONALE

Your scope of work should appear near the beginning of any research design. Start by repeating your marching orders. Your research design has to respond to and correspond with the scope of work. If the scope does not already contain language spelling out the legal and regulatory basis for the work, be sure to discuss this up front as well. This shows that you know what you are doing, and your sponsors and regulators will be comforted by the proper legal lingo. It's often easier to get your plan approved by using familiar words. It is also very important that you do understand the statutory requirements because, like it or not, you are responding to government mandate. These introductory parts set the stage for your proposed research.

PROBLEM DEFINITION

Next, your research design should explain your research context and identify your research questions. One way you can do this is to begin by reviewing the *relevant* research background—not a boiler-plate background section with a tedious chronology of every piddling project and published interpretation bearing on your research area, time period, or site type but a succinct, focused discussion of the state of knowledge about your research problem. The goal is to demonstrate that you are on top of what has already been learned or postulated concerning the research area or topic. This isn't accomplished by compiling long lists of citations but by highlighting the most important previous research and discussing the key points and critical data sets that are part of the written archaeological record (and sometimes the recent work that is not yet published). Don't just list and cite the work, but demonstrate in a cogent fashion that you have read and absorbed the importance of what your predecessors have done. The existing on-the-shelf archaeological record is a critical part of your research context.

Sometimes it is appropriate to have a section called "Theoretical (or "Conceptual") Approach" to explain where your research is coming from and where you intend it to go. Under such headings one often finds a confusing and tedious recitation of buzzwords, dense quotes, famous names, and rambling discussions of overused concepts. We've written several just like that. Make yours stand out by cutting through the fog and stating clearly and succinctly the essence of the explanation or model you are inspired by and working within. Most useful theoretical approaches have been explained well in the leading journals and academic press books. Focus on the essence. Don't parrot your sources; just cite the key references, and state the gist of the ideas. Boiling it down will win you much more respect than a lengthy and dense discussion.

In many circumstances you don't even have to discuss your theoretical approach per se. If your research is basic and aimed at addressing compliance and management issues, cut to the chase and focus on your research questions. Whatever references to established theoretical perspectives you need can be mentioned in your

"Research Background" section and in your statement of the problem. The high-church theorists need to belabor the assumptions, the history of ideas, and the abstract understandings that these views encompass as well as point us in new directions from time to time. But we rank-and-file members of the "archaeological proletariat," as Patty Jo Watson put it, have to spend more time fishing than playing with the bait.

As we said in chapter 4, research problems, hypotheses, and questions are simply different names for the same thing. One can split hairs, quote philosophers, and insist on a narrow view of how to structure scientific research, but we don't think it matters much. What does matter is that you can answer the question "What is my research intended to accomplish?" This is your problem, your hypothesis, your question. It may be little more than a basic "find and evaluate," or it may be a much more complex set of ideas. Fit your problem to the situation. Explain enough of the research context to justify why you are choosing to focus on this topic. State your research question(s) clearly.

One way to start is to lay out a central problem and then identify the parts you hope to solve. You can call these parts research questions. Or you can identify these as smaller research problems. You can start with a hypothesis—a proposed explanation of the archaeological patterning you will be investigating—and then list your expectations: what you think you will find and what you think it will mean as a test of your hypothesis. No matter how you structure your approach, the more explicit you are about what you are trying to learn, about your underlying assumptions, and about how your findings could inform your starting point, the better.

Some of the most common faults in research designs (including all of those that we have written) are that the problems are too broad, the questions are too numerous, or the hypotheses are too difficult to test. Ambition and idealism generally are good things, but they must be tempered by reality. While you do want to aim high, you also want to give yourself a realistic chance to hit the target. If your stated problem is too broad, do your best to pare it down while you are writing your research design, instead of waiting until the crucible of the field exacts its inevitable toll.

Most worthwhile research projects end up identifying more questions, narrower problems, and more sophisticated hypotheses than they started with. That is really the point of doing problem-oriented research. Starting with the best questions you can pose and focusing as narrowly and precisely as you can, you end up learning something worth knowing. In the long view one of your most important goals is to learn enough so that you (and your colleagues) can do a better job on the next research opportunity.

DATA DEFINITION

After you have explained your problem, identify the data you will need to address it. Think carefully about the data you need and can collect. You won't be able to collect all the data you need. And you'll probably collect data you won't need for your problem. Justify your data definitions by telling the reader how and why these data will (or won't) inform your problem. Justify your decisions to treat different material classes differentially by telling the reader how you've balanced the costs against the benefits. If you are going to exclude certain classes of data (as you must always do), be upfront about it. For instance, you might reason that the sherds smaller than a half inch (those that would fall through a half-inch mesh screen) are not worth bothering with because you can't learn anything from them that can't be learned from a sample of larger sherds.

You have an ethical obligation to record basic data even if these data will not inform your research questions. This means different things for different kinds of sites and different regions. You will have to meet certain standards, expectations that your colleagues, reviewers, and sponsors have established. Question these when you can and try to justify your deviations from the norm, but you can't plow through a pit house just to see whether there is a burial in its floor. You have an obligation to do a thorough job of recording the features you find and sampling the potentially meaningful deposits you encounter. You should have a plan to address these data. Explain this plan in your research design.

That said, there are circumstances in which you may decide to sacrifice basic data and normal standards to salvage something that you judge to be more important. For example, it may be justifiable to use heavy machinery to scrape off the upper deposits of a site to allow you to carefully investigate an earlier, better-preserved, and more poorly known component. Such decisions can be controversial and must be made in concert with the regulators and perhaps other parties. Such sacrifices are often necessary because you cannot do it all. By defining your critical data, you are also defining the data that are less critical in your particular circumstance.

METHODS AND TECHNIQUES

Data and methods are two sides of the same coin. To understand the data, you and your reader must understand the methods used. Most field methods are selected from a well-established array of proven techniques. You don't have to explain how you will set up a datum, grid the site, and label the bags. You do have to explain your overall methodological strategy and outline how you plan to cover the terrain on a survey, dig holes in a site, or sample a midden. If you intend to break tradition and do something methodologically innovative, take special care to elaborate and explain what you intend to do and why.

The marriage of data and methods is sometimes called your *sampling strategy*. It often helps to acknowledge that sampling pervades all archaeological research, so be explicit about your sampling methods and rationale. Why have you chosen to dig shovel tests every two hundred meters on the terrace margins? Once again, this requires your informed judgment—elaborate when you need to and be as succinct as you can. Avoid painting yourself into a no-win corner; build in contingency plans that show how your sampling strategy might change in response to field realities.

ANALYSIS

The more complex and involved your research is, the more critical it is that you discuss how you plan to analyze the data. Sometimes this section is called your "Analytical Approach." This section should flow logically from your research questions and the nature of the data; explain how you will use the data you will collect to address your questions. For basic questions, your planned analysis may be straightforward; describe and document what you found, determine how old it is, and link it to the known archaeological universe. More sophisticated questions and larger research projects will require you to develop your analytical approach in more detail. Think ahead and plan your analysis so you can budget your time and analytical expenses and so you can ensure that you collect the data your analysis will require. This step is often skipped or glossed over, usually to the detriment of the project. By including an analytical plan, you demonstrate the thoroughness of your research design and inspire confidence in your ability to complete the project within the budget.

ADDITIONAL CONSIDERATIONS

SPECIALISTS AND SPECIALIZED STUDIES

Multidisciplinary projects require close coordination, and this coordination should begin in the planning process. If you plan to use specialists or perform specialized studies, you should address these needs in each relevant section of your research design. For example, you may need to hire a historian to search for scattered records that pertain to the construction of structures once present in your study area. Mention the data you hope to collect in the data definition section, and describe the methods to be used to collect those data. In the analysis section, discuss your specific analytical approach to the data. Specialists may be at another institution and you may never meet face-to-face, so they need a well-crafted research design to understand how their work fits into your overall approach. By anticipating and discussing the specialists' roles in your analysis, your research design will pave the way toward a successful collaboration.

ANTICIPATING COMPLICATIONS

As you assemble your document, do your best to anticipate and discuss the normal kinds of complications that may arise: inclement weather; the hoped-for data fail to materialize; there is not enough water to do water screening; you encounter human remains. Describe briefly your contingency plan for dealing with these difficulties. By doing this explicitly, your research design will show your sponsors that you've got a foot in the real world, and it will provide a handy "plan B" to fall back on when things threaten to fall apart.

If you encounter human remains, you will probably have to follow a specific protocol that varies greatly depending on your source of funding, the ownership of the land, the age and cultural affiliation of the burial, and the region of the country you are in (see sidebar 7.3). In many circumstances, you will need to consult with appropriate tribal authorities and consider their concerns. In some cases, you may

7.3. NAGPRA

Some of the most contentious issues and greatest confusions in modern American archaeology revolve around the Native American Graves Protection and Repatriation Act (NAGPRA) of 1990. This law essentially says that human graves on federal and tribal lands are to be protected and that Native American descendants should decide the fate of the bones, grave goods, and sacred objects of their ancestors that are encountered or held by the federal government and any institution that receives federal money. The law and its regulations also set up a repatriation process. NAGPRA basically tries to balance the very real concerns and legitimate interests of Native Americans in controlling their cultural patrimony with the scientific community's interests in studying and preserving these materials. For most working CRM folks and academic field archaeologists as well, NAGPRA can impact your work in two ways.

First, if you're doing archaeology on federal or tribal lands, you need to ensure that the appropriate tribes or Native Hawaiian organizations have been consulted, usually before the work begins. It is the sponsoring organization's responsibility to consult, but don't leave it up to them. You should be part of the consultation process. The consultation should spell out what happens if any human remains or burial goods are uncovered as part of your work. You may need to stop work and call in a tribal representative. Or you may need to handle burials and grave goods according to a specific protocol. The key is to follow the law

have to quit digging or avoid any human remains entirely. In others, you may need to have a physical anthropologist examine the remains in the field and then immediately turn them over to a Native American group for reburial. If you don't know the protocol in your area, consult with your SHPO or sponsoring agency. Thinking ahead is far better than dealing with an ugly and costly crisis. Outline your plan for such contingencies in your research design.

RESPONDING TO THE SCOPE OF WORK

Your research design should be written and organized in ways that are directly responsive to the scope of work. Make sure that your research plan fits within the scope and that you have satisfied the concerns and needs of your sponsor and your regulators. This may mean being certain that you include certain language or certain sections that are expected or required. This is particularly critical if your research design is part of your proposal for a competitive bid. RFPs that

and all appropriate procedures. NAGPRA is the law, and the law says that federally recognized tribes have a legitimate interest in the remains of their ancestors.

The second way you may find yourself under the NAGPRA umbrella is when human remains or grave goods are encountered in the course of a federally funded or permitted archaeological project that is not located on federal or tribal land. State laws and procedures will generally apply, even on private property, but NAGPRA will control the disposition of Native American human remains and certain objects if they are held by a federal agency or federally funded institution. Know your state burial laws as well as NAGPRA. What you have to do will again depend on where you are and who is sponsoring and permitting your work. Your best bet is to contact your SHPO and federal sponsor and follow their advice.

For the most part, NAGPRA works reasonably well. Most of the archaeological community seems to be taking NAGPRA in stride and complying with the law. But it's complicated and contentious, particularly when it comes to the numerous "culturally unaffiliated" remains that cannot be clearly linked to a living tribe, like virtually all of those that are thousands of years old. Over a decade after NAGPRA's enactment, the final regulations for treatment of these remains still have not been approved.

Handling NAGPRA-related situations requires consultation, compromise, and the willingness to work within established protocol. Accommodating NAGPRA and making productive use of its challenges and opportunities in both the field and the lab is part of your successful research strategy.

are written by archaeological bureaucrats may mandate that you follow a particular document format, keep to a certain length, address certain problems, or even follow a particular methodology. You may find such directives maddening and even nonsensical, but you will probably have a better chance of winning the contract if you bite your tongue and follow the guidelines. "Nonresponsive" proposals may be summarily dismissed, even if your objections are reasonable. If you do choose to buck the system and propose an alternative approach, explain your reasoning carefully and noncontentiously. Sometimes it's better to negotiate such deviations after you have the contract in hand.

Responding to the scope of work is really a matter of thinking about who will be reading your research design and anticipating their needs, concerns, and likely responses. Your sponsor or client may not care about your research plan except insofar as it affects the schedule or the budget. Your regulators may not care about scheduling and budgets but may be quite picky about your proposed methods. There is no precise formula for success—you have to create the document that does what is needed in your situation. By carefully reading and rereading the scope of work and making sure your research design is consistent with the scope, you can save yourself lots of unneeded hassle. Don't forget that your peers may be keenly interested in your research design for a variety of reasons. Don't be paranoid, but do try to look at your document from the vantage point of the devil's advocate. How will it read to your professional colleagues?

CONCLUSION

Your written research design spells out just a part of what you will have to do. Most of your operational strategy won't be part of the written document. But it is no less a part of your plan, so don't let it go unheeded. If you've prepared a logistics checklist, grab that now, print a clean copy of your research design, and put those two documents together in a binder or a folder, or paste them in the back of your field book. Just as your logistics checklist is a guide to the mundane, everyday crap that has to be done, your research design is a guide to the legal, regulatory, and intellectual things that need to be done. One won't do you much good without the other.

8

PUTTING YOUR RESEARCH DESIGN TO WORK

Your research design is done, you've got the contract or grant in hand, and now it's time to do the archaeology you've designed. Your research design is a tool, and if you leave it hidden in your toolbox while you're working, it won't help you.

The process of designing your research has forced you to think first. Your research design provides a very real research context that helps you collect data and make observations with the confidence of knowing how this information will help you answer your research questions. You've already considered many of the decisions you will have to make in the field and laid out a reasonable course of action—your archaeological and operational strategies. You've already done the work in your mind, by going through the process of designing your research. With a written research design in your hands, you and your crew have a map to success.

Yet, the unexpected will always arise. When new things pop up that you're not prepared for, the first tool you should grab is your research design. How does the new situation affect the data you're collecting? Is this new data? How does it fit into the analytical model? What changes will it mean to other parts of the data collection and analysis effort? Handling change intelligently is one of the hardest tasks in any endeavor, and your research design provides a structure to handle—and incorporate—those changes in your overall research plan.

Even after the work is done, the analysis is complete, and the report is almost in the bag, your research design is still at work. The last, and most important step—for you—is using your research design to honestly evaluate your work. Looking back on what worked and what didn't, assessing what you would do differently and how you could do better, is how you become a better researcher and archaeologist. Your research design provides not only a structure for your research but a structure for your professional growth.

IMPLEMENTING YOUR RESEARCH DESIGN

Your research design does a very simple thing: It communicates. It codifies the things you hope to learn from the archaeological record; the kinds of data you expect to collect; the ways you plan to collect, record, and manage that data; and the approaches you'll use to analyze those data. It also communicates those things to the people working with you, your sponsors, and regulators. Archaeological projects, even small ones, are complex undertakings, and your research design helps keep you on track and moving in (hopefully) the right direction. Clear communication is the key to effectively implementing your research design.

SHARING THE DREAM

Once you get the green light on your research project, the first thing you should do with your research design is to share it with others, especially the members of your research team. The element of surprise might be useful in battle, but it can be death for an archaeological project. Everyone involved in your project needs to know your approach, the data you hope to collect, and how you hope to collect it. That's just what your research design does. Suggest that the crew read your research design, and, if possible, set aside time for discussion. Don't forget any specialists who will be involved in your research or analysis. When the members of your research team know the context of the research they are undertaking, they become more active and helpful participants.

One part of active participation that some archaeologists have a hard time dealing with is criticism from the crew. It can be disconcerting to expose your ideas and plans to the folks who work for you. The crew might criticize or laugh at your plans, but so what? This is the real world of research—if the crew sees flaws in your work, you can be confident that your peers will as well. Look at this as an opportunity to make your research design and project better. It could be that you've just done a poor job of communicating, that your ideas aren't clearly explained. There's no better way to clarify your thoughts than to try to explain them to someone who doesn't understand. If you're honest with them, respect their criticisms, and use the opportunity to benefit from their experience, you'll have a team with a common goal. If you're hesitant to accept criticism from the those who work for you, how are you going to feel when the report comes out for everybody to read? Evaluation, criticism, and comparison are standard stock in the CRM trade.

Look for opportunities to share your research design with colleagues and peers, too. If colleagues express an interest in visiting your site, invite them, and send them a copy of your research design before the visit. Sometimes this can seem like asking for a poke in the eye with a sharp stick—expect colleagues to point out problems they see and tell you how they would do things. Differences of opinion are to be expected, but they may also call your attention to alternatives you haven't considered, changes you may want to implement right away. No matter what the tone, your colleagues' first impressions can be very valuable feedback. Hear them out, record their observations and concerns in your notes, and use these later during your analysis and write-up to help you strengthen your arguments and explain your case.

FOLLOWING THROUGH

One of the challenges of fieldwork is following through on what you proposed in the research design. This seems obvious and simple but seldom is. In the field or the lab, it's easy to fall back into familiar default patterns—deeply ingrained habits. So use your research design to assess the work you're doing at each stage of your research. A good approach is to do a quick weekly evaluation. Look at your research design—really look at it, don't rely on your memory—get the thing out and review what you said you'd be doing at this stage. Have you revised your data collection methods because of special soil conditions? Even seemingly trivial changes in your methods could mean that you're not collecting the data you expected. Even if your crew members have read and discussed your plan, they, too, may backslide into old habits. If you're using forms to collect systematic observations in the field and lab, you need to review them and make sure that the observations recorded are what you expected. When forms are filled out in a rote fashion, the real variability often gets hidden behind a wall of convenience. A quick weekly review of those data can help you head off those problems. It might be that you weren't as clear as you needed to be, and a quick explanation could fix the problem.

Review the status of your project, your data, and your research design on a regular schedule. On large projects you might be required to produce a regular monthly status report, which is a great opportunity to review what you're doing and how it fits within your research plan. Even if there's no requirement in your contract, it's a good idea for you to perform a regular status check. And it's not enough to just mentally check off what you're doing. Our perception is wonderfully imprecise, and our memories are often conveniently unreliable. You should actually sit down with your research design, spend an hour or so reviewing the work, and make sure that you're staying on track. And write it down! Just a section in your notes is fine, but by writing down your impressions, you create a valuable record of your progress (or lack thereof) that you can look back at during the analysis and write-up.

Sounds like a good idea, you say, but when do I find the time? You won't, unless you build time into your schedule to handle the chore. Maybe you set aside an hour every Friday morning or chop an hour out of Wednesday afternoon. Review and reflection comprise a critical part of any research process, and, if you build them into your project, you'll be a better researcher for it.

WORKING WITH SPECIALISTS

The specialists and those who provide analytical services instrumental to your research design will need special consideration. Those who take part in the fieldwork will obviously need to be scheduled appropriately. For example, the best time for geoarchaeology may be early in the field season if you need depositional interpretation to guide your work or late in the field season if the work depends on maximum excavation exposure. Don't pass up any opportunity to invite the specialists who will do their work later to come visit you in the field. This exposure (plus reading your research design) will give them the contextual information crucial to the success of many specialized studies. Keep in mind that most specialists have their own research agendas that may be quite different from yours. If you don't make it clear what you want from them, they will often give you what they perceive as important instead of what you need. For example, faunal experts who aren't archaeologists may concentrate on identifying species and elements and may not make systematic observations about evidence of modification (butchering marks, burning, gnawing, etc.). With careful coordination, you will be able to integrate your specialists into your research.

WHEN THE PLAN HITS THE FAN

No matter how well you plan, your research design will start to fall apart shortly after you hit the field. Hopefully, you'll just have small problems that nibble away at the edges of your work, like fire-cracked rocks that are too large to be weighed on the field scale you intended to use or aerial photographs that don't show the roads you had counted on using to locate your survey quadrants. The more you count on a perfect field season with everything falling into place just at the right moment, the more likely you'll end up scrambling to finish something that only vaguely resembles what you set out to do. Big or small, problems will occur, and to keep your sanity and your research design intact, you need to plan for failure.

Planning for failure doesn't mean having a contingency plan for every possible disaster. It means approaching problems the same way you approach your research: by thinking first. When you encounter unexpected circumstances, take a step back. Think. If you can use something from your plan to help solve the problem, great. But remember that reality takes precedence. Always. It's not what we want or hope or expect that counts, it's what's there. When you encounter a major logistical problem or an unanticipated archaeological circumstance, the key is to react to it intelligently.

Your research design is a tool for decision making, but only if you believe in it. That is, if you have a well-focused problem and good research questions, do your best to stay on track. When unanticipated wrinkles appear, look to your research design to help you make decisions. How can you accommodate the new situation and still address all or most of your research questions? Remember that failure is not the only thing you'll have to prepare for. Sometimes unexpected success can cause even more problems. You're digging along and suddenly an unexpected and time-consuming feature pops up. Halfway through your survey you realize that your team is finding twice as many sites as you predicted and time is running out. Your excavation of an eighteenth-century house turns up a previously unrecognized prehistoric component rich with promise. What do you do: stick with your game plan, or go for the newfound glory?

We don't often think of archaeology as an experimental science, but it is. Each time we take to the field and drop our shovel into the dirt, we're experimenting. We have an expectation of what we might find and how we're going to deal with it. When we find something unexpected, it's not because we've failed; our experiment is simply showing us new information. Our job, then, is to pause and rethink our strategy to incorporate this new circumstance.

Stop. Think. Think again. You are right back to making tough decisions and weighing costs against benefits as you consider revising your strategy based on the new circumstances. You have three choices: Stick with your original plan, modify your plan to accommodate the new situation, or scrap your plan entirely and come up with a new one. You should consider the latter option only in truly extraordinary circumstances. If you ditch your original plan, you'll need to create a new research design, and you will almost certainly need approval from the powers that be; otherwise, you won't be fulfilling the contract or the terms of your permit. If you abandon your plan and start making ad hoc reactionary decisions on your own without a comprehensive strategy and without approval, you are begging for trouble and are right back to archaeology by default.

Sometimes you may decide to stick with your game plan, keeping your original focus and ignoring the new opportunity. You know you can't do everything, and sometimes staying on course may be the most reasonable alternative, particularly if your sponsor isn't willing to give you the extra time or funding needed to do more than you originally planned. But often you will want to shift your priorities and take advantage of the unexpected.

As long as you approach these things intelligently, handling change in the field isn't too difficult. It's the same as if you had found some new information when you were working on your research design. Look at the new circumstance; see how it impacts your research design. Start by asking yourself these questions:

- How does this change the data I expected to collect?
- What are these new or changed data?
- Do I need to modify my methods to collect the data?
- How can I analyze these data to inform my research questions?
- Do I need to revise or create new research questions to accommodate these data?
- How will this impact the rest of the project in time and money?

As you review these questions, develop a plan for addressing the change, and write it down. You can start this process in your notes, but plan to get the changes down more formally as quickly as possible. This is the research design process all over, but instead of starting from scratch, you've got the work you've already done in hand, and you're just adding a new wrinkle. Of course, you've got a crew standing around waiting, a sponsor anxious to get moving, and three weeks left in your schedule, so you can't spend a lot of time digesting this new information. Using the questions listed earlier, specify—in writing—what the problem or potential is and how you propose to handle it.

As you document your changes, remember that your research design is a record of your approach to the work. Think of the research design as intellectual field notes. Although you don't want to re-create your research design as each change or problem comes along, you do want to document the process you went through to get to the final stage. If you change your methods in the field, add a section to your research design explaining the change and why it was made. Don't simply replace the original information with your revision. That's dishonest. You need to know why you made the changes, and so do your readers.

If you're revising your approach, you must work with your sponsor and regulators to make them aware of any changes to your plan and make sure they concur. If the revised plan is more costly in time or money, you obviously must get the OK before preceding. Often the easiest way to gain their approval is to invite them to visit you in the field and see the new circumstances for themselves. Hand them a copy of your proposed changes, explain your case, accommodate their suggestions, and try to get everybody on board the new and improved plan.

Verbal agreements aren't enough—you need to get this stuff in writing. Write a quick memo or letter reviewing the meeting and who was there, noting that "On XX date we agreed that. . . ." Make sure you spell out the proposed changes to your research design, and fax or mail it to all of the involved parties. Communication, again, is the key. In tense or potentially contentious circumstances, you may want to ask for signed acknowledgment. If contractual obligations change, you may need a formal contract amendment. This annoying paperwork will seem like manna from heaven if contract disputes arise later and you have a paper trail supporting your version of events.

Documenting any changes you make also keeps your crew and specialists on the same page. Whenever changes are made in the field, it's critical that everyone who will be affected, from the field tech in the bottom of the trench to the plant specialist four states away, knows and understands what the change is and how it will affect the data to be collected and analyzed. The quickest, most effective way to do that is to hand them a couple of sheets of paper, let them read it, and talk about what it means. It's simple and it works, and if you don't do it, you may screw yourself.

Documenting these changes is most important to you. When you're knee deep in the analysis or write-up, the last thing you need is to confront ill-remembered problems in the data. When you find six bags of stuff that you vaguely remember were pulled from some hole, somewhere, for some reason, the cold pit in the bottom of your stomach will quickly disappear if you can turn to your notes and jog your memory.

IN FROM THE COLD

Often the time you really have to face reality isn't in the field but when you get back to the lab. You should have been revisiting your research design at each step of the process, but let's be realistic. You may not have recognized (or been able or willing to recognize) that the data you needed to address your research questions just weren't there. Once you're back in the lab, trying to fit the data into your analysis, it may quickly become apparent that there is no way you can address half of your research questions. What do you do—scrap the research design and hope that no one else will go back and read it?

No, this is just another problem to overcome. Don't panic. Use your research design. Look at your research questions in light of the data you've actually collected. Where the data can be applied to your proposed questions, do it. You may not have the whole answer, you may not have all the data, but just say that and move on. If some of your data don't match what you proposed, document it. Write it down, right now. Describe the data and the methods, as accurately as possible. Look at the data in terms of your current questions; there may be places where the data can be applied. If there doesn't seem to be a fit between your data and your research questions, you may need to propose an alternative set of questions or problems. If you do, write them down, and consult with your sponsor and regulators. Remember, revising your research design means adding new information and explaining your changes, not providing a revisionist view of your work. Once you've made your revisions, get those folks to sign off on the changes.

THE LAB STAFF CAN READ, TOO

In the happy event that you return from the field with the targeted data and your research questions still more or less intact, use your research design to prioritize the lab processing and focus your analysis. As with your field crew and specialists, your first step in the lab should be to provide all of the staff with copies of your research design. Spend some time with them discussing the fieldwork completed, the lab work to come, and the looming analysis. Don't let default routines and ad hoc decisions prevent you from reaching your research objectives. The same process that applies in the field also applies in the lab. If you encounter problems, approach them with research design in hand, systematically, and document any changes you might need to make. Keep focused and keep using your research design to guide the work. By sticking with your game plan, you might even be able to save enough time to follow "bonus" research leads that turn up in the course of your work. But keep your priorities straight—follow through on your research design.

ORGANIZING YOUR REPORT

Your research design (as revised) provides you with a logical and compelling organizational structure for your report. Screw the tedious boilerplate and mindless detail—you have the perfect justification to prepare your report in creative and unique ways. Start by laying out your research design, and then structure the report to follow your design to its logical conclusion. If you've followed your research plan, you have sets of data that address specific questions. Lay out your report just like that. When you do problem-oriented research, when you use a research design to guide your work, what you have to report is fundamentally different from the standard CRM fare. You do have the usual compliance crap to regurgitate—so many acres, so many shovel tests. But more important and interesting, you have a set of assertions and the data needed to test them, so you can create compelling arguments about aspects of the archaeological record. Do what you must to satisfy the regulators and the sponsor, but then look back at your research questions and lay out your data, methods, and analysis, and then address the research questions you posed. You've learned something, something about the archaeological record, something about archaeological methods, something about floodproofing your excavation block. Give that to the reader, to your colleagues.

EVALUATING YOUR RESEARCH DESIGN

As the analysis and writing phase draws to a close, the final step of any thorough research program is to evaluate the research design. What worked and what didn't? Which of the grandly stated ideas were you able to effectively test or address with the data in hand? What happened with the other ideas, the ones you could not effectively address? Did all of your methods and analytical strategies pay off? Faced with a similar circumstance, how could you improve on your research design?

Sadly, many of us fail to truly evaluate and honestly judge the effectiveness of our research designs. We tend to scrap the ideas that our data don't speak to and focus on the research questions we can address. Fine enough, but we also tend to skip the crucial step of sitting down and admitting to ourselves and others what worked and what didn't. We gloss over (or completely ignore) our mistakes as if admitting error were tantamount to admitting professional incompetence. Failing to learn from our mistakes, or at least failing to share what we have learned, we doom ourselves and others to repeat our mistakes. We forget that archaeological research is a cumulative and cyclical process and that the point of making mistakes should be to learn from them.

Your research design is a tool for learning about both the archaeological record and the process of doing archaeology. Sections labeled "Interpretations" or "Conclusion" in archaeological reports say something about what we think we have learned. Don't stop there. You should also specifically discuss the effectiveness of your research design. Which lines of evidence and research strategies were helpful? Proudly tout the ideas and strategies that worked, but keep in mind that they only tell a part of the overall story. Equally important are the ideas and strategies that didn't work. By discussing these shortfalls, you (and others as well) can learn from your mistakes.

It's natural to try to avoid talking about what we might see as our failures. But no project is perfect, and the picture presented by many CRM reports—where it seems the work went smoothly (except for weather) and the analysis was flawless—is sheer fantasy. We all know that all kinds of problems crop up, that none of our data sets is without flaws, and that it's difficult to usefully analyze archaeological data. Learning about the archaeological record means sharing information, good, bad, and indifferent.

Consider adding a section to your report called "Evaluating the Research Design." Work through your research design, point by point. Look at your research questions, your methods, the data you hoped to collect, and your analysis. Ask yourself (and answer) these questions about each part of the research design:

- Did this work?
- Did we encounter problems with this in the field, lab, or analysis?
- Did we revise it?
- If it was revised, did that fix the problem?
- How could this be made better or more effective?

The goal here isn't self-flagellation, but be as honest as you can. Don't apologize or make excuses. The goal is to evaluate each section dispassionately. If you've been documenting changes to your research design as you've gone along, point out how and why things changed. Remember, your research design is really a process. Evaluating it completes the cycle.

There are no perfect research designs. Understanding what worked and what didn't will help you do a better job next time. Owning up to half-baked ideas and ineffective strategies is one of the basic obligations of an ethical researcher. It will also help other archaeologists understand the work you did and hopefully avoid some of the traps you found. It will enhance your reputation as forthright researcher. It's your obligation to learn something from the time and money that your archaeological research project has swallowed. Learning what not to do next time is as critical as learning what worked. Report the truth.

NOW IT'S UP TO YOU

Excellent and meaningful archaeological research is being accomplished every day by archaeologists all across the country. There's also much that is overpriced, mindless, and mercenary being done under the banner of "archaeology." The path you'll take is up to you.

The road to accomplishing excellent research in archaeology—CRM or academic—is anything but easy. The money and the opportunities are there in the CRM world, but the pace is often relentless. When and where you work will be determined by engineering concerns, bureaucratic decisions, market factors, political winds, and construction schedules. Your research has to focus where and when these larger forces say, and you have to make it fit within the framework of federal, state, and local preservation laws and regulations. You'll share archaeological decision making with government archaeologists who work as contract managers, reviewers, and regulators and with many interested parties who aren't archaeologists. There will be compromises at every turn, and some of them will turn you inside out. None of us survives for long in the research world with all of our academic ideals intact. Reality always takes precedence.

It's no wonder that the academic world disparages CRM archaeology. It's damn hard to do good research with all of these pressures and constraints. When your research arena is defined by others, you must be opportunistic, persistent, and resourceful. No one likes to think and work with people hanging over her shoulder, yet the whole archaeological bureaucracy is designed around just that concept, and you can't begrudge the need for accountability in publicly funded work. The upshot is that CRM archaeologists simply don't have control over big chunks of their research world.

In spite of this, CRM archaeologists are making substantive contributions to the archaeological record, day in and day out. One of the things that CRM archaeology does is force us to look outside our usual box. What, for instance, would we know about upland sites without CRM archaeology? If the archaeologists were doing the choosing, we'd all be down in the deep sandy loam up to our armpits in stratigraphy. But because the engineers who route the pipelines, highways, and power grids choose our work locations, we've been looking at these thin, shallow, and interestingly different sites for the last thirty years. Just the fact that CRM projects have forced us to deal with such "marginal" (and numerous) sites on the landscape is an important contribution to archaeology. Being told where to work isn't all bad.

It's hard, though, to do interesting research consistently when you're faced with a nonstop stream of small surveys and testing jobs. It's a formidable challenge to you as a researcher, a much greater challenge than excavating a well-stratified site. Your professional objective is the same: to make a useful and interesting contribution to the archaeological record. The logistical and practical problems are immense: short projects, small areas, and few truly significant archaeologically deposits. The retreat into archaeology by default is easy to understand. The same projects, the same analyses, the same reports. It's a hard trap to escape, even when you're determined.

The worst part of the bittersweet reward for enduring the trap is that you become someone who can be counted on to accomplish the technical routine. Not creative, but reliable. The work gets done and the report goes in on time. You won't want for work, but no one will want to read your reports, not even you. The only punishable crimes are to badly overspend your budget, seriously inconvenience the construction schedule, or miss your final due date. The real problem with CRM archaeology is that the easiest path leads to a dreary, soulless technical service.

It doesn't have to be that way. By choosing to do archaeology by design, by carefully thinking about the archaeology, by doing problem-driven research while meeting your compliance obligations, you can make your work exciting, interesting, and meaningful. You have to take a long view of your research. It's not what you find that counts; it's how the data you collect, the methods you use, and the approach you take give you and your colleagues a leg up on the next one. It's also having a research perspective, a plan to carry it out, and the gumption to report what you really did and learned.

The only consistent route to doing interesting, effective, problem-driven research is through the process of designing your research. It's a proven method that we archaeologists and social scientists borrowed from the hard sciences. For all the preaching and proclaiming we've done in these pages, the process itself is pretty simple. First, you have to recognize and grasp the opportunity. Next, you have to have a research perspective, something you care about and are interested in studying. Then, given the work at hand, think about questions you can ask and imagine the data you can collect and how it will help you address those questions. The rest is window dressing, creative (or dull) variations on a theme. The key, though, is simple: Think about your research perspective, problems, and data, and do archaeology by design.

This book is meant to be a guide to helping you learn how to create successful strategies for achieving substantive archaeological research. Our views are shaped by many painful mistakes made and witnessed in the real world of archaeology. It's up to you to glean what you can from these pages and adapt it to the actual circumstances you find yourself in. You will make many of the same mistakes we made. Despite knowing in theory what you should do, in practice you will find yourself caught with not enough time or money or willpower to do the right thing.

Your attitude, skills, and aptitude will determine whether you accomplish archaeological research of consequence during your career.

If you pursue opportunities with eyes wide open and heart and mind set on doing research, your career in archaeology will count for something more than a road to retirement.

Your written research design is often an important part of the process, but most of what it will take will go unwritten. It will take knowledge (much of it acquired on your own), relevant skills, and on-the-job training. It will take a good command of all the interrelated contexts of your work, from politics to the physical and cultural landscape to logistics. It will take a willingness to make the most of thankless situations. A keen sense of humor helps—archaeological research is a surreal world at times, and you'd better be able to appreciate irony and absurdity (it's either that or pulling your hair out). It will take interpersonal skills, from ego stroking to consensus building to learning how to say, "You're fired." It will take tempering your ideals with a heavy dose of pragmatism—you may have to sacrifice large chunks of the in-the-ground archaeological record in order to learn and to save its most significant parts. It will take many, many tough decisions. And on and on. It's all part of the tangled process of designing archaeological research.

The need to be purposeful in your research cannot be overemphasized. In most projects, you won't have the luxury or mandate to protect all sites or take your sweet time doing everything that can be done. Faced with finite resources and ticking time, you must be purposeful and focus your research.

Doing archaeology by design gives you and your organization a competitive advantage. When you focus your research on specific problems of consequence, you accomplish more of substance for a given amount of money. Archaeology by default is expensive even if you are merely going through the motions, doing your fieldwork in the usual way, and collecting, processing, reporting, and curating forever whatever you happen to find. The costs mount up in such an unfocused approach, and the payoff is always uncertain. When you focus your work, you can spend the money more productively because you know what you're after and what you can do without. It's just smart business to concentrate on achieving something worthwhile. Smart business, smart archaeology—and that is the secret to archaeology by design.

Now, it's up to you.

APPENDIX A

 # GROUPS YOU SHOULD JOIN

The results of your archaeological work join the body of work that we all draw on when we try to understand the archaeological record. You are part of a profession, a discipline, a cohort of archaeologists who contribute to that body of work. The more active a role you take in thinking, talking, and writing about archaeology, the better an archaeologist you will be. To do these things, you need to interact with other archaeologists, folks who will listen to what you have to say and challenge you and your ideas, folks who can inspire you, and folks who you can inspire. Anthropology has a word for such interacting groups—*societies*.

Society for American Archaeology (SAA)
900 Second Street NE, #12
Washington, D.C. 20002-3557
Phone: (202) 789-8200
Fax: (202) 789-0284
headquarters@saa.org
www.saa.org

Every archaeologist in North America should join the Society for American Archaeology, the largest and most influential national group. In addition to publishing *American Antiquity*, *Latin American Antiquity*, and the *SAA Archaeological Record*, the SAA provides access to a variety of resources and a national forum for presenting ideas. There is no better way to get a sense of where your work fits into the larger body of archaeology than at the SAA's annual meeting each spring. Although the SAA has been traditionally dominated by academic archaeologists, CRM archaeologists are assuming greater roles at every level of the organization. This shift is reflected in the content of the the *SAA Archaeological Record* and in the SAA's backing of ROPA, the Register of Professional Archaeologists.

Register of Professional Archaeologists (ROPA)
5024-R Campbell Blvd.
Baltimore, Maryland 21236
Phone: (410) 933-3486
www.rpanet.org

ROPA is a listing of professional archaeologists in the United States who have agreed to abide by an explicit code of conduct and standards of research performance; who hold a graduate degree in archaeology, anthropology, or other germane discipline; and who have substantial practical experience. ROPA was established in 1998, jointly sponsored by the SAA, the Society for Historical Archaeology (SHA), the Archaeological Institute of America (AIA), and the Society of Professional Archaeologists (SOPA). ROPA succeeds SOPA, a group that tried with only modest success to promote professional accreditation since 1976. The joint sponsorship has already resulted in a much larger membership as archaeologists around the country, academic and CRM, are recognizing the advantages of becoming a registered professional archaeologist (RPA). The hope is that a majority of professional archaeologists in the United States will join ROPA and provide our profession with the means to police itself effectively as others do. Do your part—earn your ROPA credentials by gaining the experience and graduate degree you'll need for career advancement.

If you have an area of specialization within archaeology, you should also join appropriate professional organizations such as these:

Society of Historical Archaeology (SHA)
PO Box 30446
Tucson, Arizona 85751-0446
www.sha.org

American Association of Physical Anthropologists (AAPA)
AAPA Membership
Box 1897
Lawrence, Kansas 66044-8897
physanth.org

Society of Archaeological Sciences
c/o Felicia R. Beardsley
Department of Anthropology
University of California–Riverside
Riverside, California 92521-0418
Phone: (909) 787-5524
Fax: (909) 787-5409
E-mail: beardsley@qnet.com
www.wisc.edu/larch/sas/sas.htm

Regional societies and conferences also should form an important part of your archaeological world. Here are a few, but check with your SHPO or professors for the ones in your area.

Plains Anthropological Society
Southeastern Archaeological Conference
Pecos Conference
Mid-Atlantic Archaeological Conference
Mogollon Conference
Caddo Conference

As for groups specializing in CRM, most states now have professional archaeological councils made up mainly of CRM archaeologists. These groups provide important opportunities for professional networking. Your SHPO or the SAA's Council of Councils can give you the right contacts.

The American Cultural Resources Association (ACRA) functions as a trade organization and has become an important forum and lobby for the CRM industry. It also has an excellent Listserv, ACRA-L, and a good website with many useful links.

American Cultural Resources Association (ACRA)
Thomas R. Wheaton
Executive Director, ACRA
6150 East Ponce de Leon Avenue
Stone Mountain, Georgia 30083
www.acra-crm.org

Every CRM archaeologist should be concerned about the preservation of the archaeological record and public support for archaeology. You can play a direct role by participating in state and local archaeological societies and associations. Some societies are strictly collector oriented. But many strong, successful societies engage professionals and avocational archaeologists as well as students and other enthusiasts. Those groups that welcome professional participation often have cadres of avocational archaeologists as knowledgeable of their local areas as any archaeologist alive and eager to share their insights. They can be invaluable sources of information, inspiration, support, and trained help, but it only works when it's a two-way partnership. The societies look to professionals for leadership, training, and knowledge, which we should be glad to provide.

You can't afford the cost in time and money to join and participate in all the archaeology-related groups you might want to, so prioritize them and stay involved with a few. Your membership dues, conference trips, and other expenses can be deducted from your taxes as professional business expenses.

APPENDIX B

 # JOURNALS YOU SHOULD READ

Dozens of archaeological journals, newsletters, and magazines can keep you up-to-date. You can't afford to subscribe to all of them, and even if you could, you'd never have enough time to read all of them regularly. But don't let this stop you from trying because keeping abreast of the field is essential to being a well-informed professional. Here are some strategies that might work for you.

Subscribe to as many archaeology-related serial publications as you can reasonably afford. This is your livelihood, and subscription costs are tax-deductible. The journals are much easier to refer to if you have them on your bookshelf. Some are free. You can gain access to the others by borrowing them from colleagues or spending a few hours in the library from time to time. Increasingly, journals and magazines are putting abstracts or entire contents online. Browse their websites when you can. For paper journals, scan the table of contents of each issue, and put a sticky note on all the articles you should read. If the journal is not yours, scan the articles of interest and copy the most important ones (five or ten cents a page is cheap for reference material). Keep a stack of flagged journals and copied articles in your favorite reading places, and read the articles as you have a chance. Try not to let the stack build up too high. Set aside a couple of quiet reading lunches each week. Two articles a week is more than a hundred a year. Keeping current with your field is a discipline you need to develop and nurture.

Here is a list of archaeological and related journals of international, national, and regional scope; you'll have to find the state and other regional ones for yourself.

American Anthropologist—flagship journal of the American Anthropological Association

American Antiquity—flagship journal of the Society for American
Archaeology; a must

American Archaeology—quarterly from the Archaeological Conser-
vancy

Archaeology—popular articles on sexy archaeology worldwide

Common Ground—The federal archaeology viewpoint quarterly from
the National Park Service (NPS)

CRM—another overdesigned rah-rah rag produced by the NPS, but
free

Current Anthropology—in-depth academic articles and commentary

Geoarchaeology—for the subdiscipline

Historical Archaeology—flagship journal of the Society for Historical
Archaeology

Human Ecology—interdisciplinary academic journal

International Journal of Historical Archaeology—academic

Journal of Anthropological Archaeology—a theory-heavy academic

Journal of Archaeological Method and Theory—academic topical
syntheses

Journal of Archaeological Research—academic topical reviews

Journal of Archaeological Science—archaeometry, published in the
United Kingdom

Journal of Field Archaeology—academic focusing on methods and results

Journal of Material Culture—interdisciplinary academic journal

The Kiva—regional journal focusing on the American Southwest

Latin American Antiquity—second journal of the Society for American Archaeology

Lithic Technology—specialist journal

Mammoth Trumpet—Paleo-Indian research newsletter with in-depth
interviews

Midcontinental Journal of Archaeology—regional journal

North American Archaeologist—not as impressive as its title, but im-
proving

Plains Anthropologist—regional journal

Public Archaeology—new journal produced in the United Kingdom

Public Archaeology Review—small journal focused on CRM archaeology

Quaternary Research—interdisciplinary academic journal emphasizing paleoenvironments

APPENDIX C

THE ABCs OF CRM

Modern archaeology is rife with acronyms. You can't avoid them, so you might as well learn them. Here are a few of the most common ones:

ACHP—Advisory Council on Historic Preservation
ACRA—American Cultural Resources Association
AHPA—Archeological and Historical Preservation Act (of 1974), a.k.a. Moss-Bennett
APE—area of potential effect
ARPA—Archeological Resources Protection Act (of 1979)
BLM—Bureau of Land Management
COE—U.S. Army Corps of Engineers (also USACE)
CRM—Cultural Resource Management
EO 11593—Executive Order 11593 (of 1972)
MOA—memorandum of agreement
MOU—memorandum of understanding
NAGPRA—Native American Graves Protection and Repatriation Act (of 1990)
NCSHPO—National Conference of State Historic Preservation Officers
NEH—National Endowment for the Humanities
NEPA—National Environmental Policy Act (of 1969)
NHPA—National Historic Preservation Act (of 1966)
NPS—National Park Service
NRHP—National Register of Historic Places
NSF—National Science Foundation

PMOA—programmatic memorandum of agreement
RFP—request for proposals
ROPA—Register of Professional Archaeologists
RPA—registered professional archaeologist (accredited by ROPA)
SAA—Society for American Archaeology
SHA—Society for Historical Archaeology
SHPO—State Historic Preservation Office (and officer); pronounced "ship-oh"
TCP—traditional cultural property
THPO—Tribal Historic Preservation Office (and officer); pronounced "tip-oh"

APPENDIX D

 THE LOGISTICS CHECKLIST

L ogistics can kill a project. If you're fifteen miles and forty-five minutes from town when you use your last collection bag, or the batteries for your TDS aren't charged, or someone forgets to gas the truck, it's not just you who will be twiddling thumbs. It's expensive to field even a small crew, and every hour they sit on their hands because something they need isn't available is eight or ten hours you've lost in the lab or the analysis or the write-up. Good logistics doesn't necessarily mean good archeology, but bad logistics can kill any hope you have to finish a project on time and within budget.

Luckily for us administratively challenged folks, there is a miracle tool that can virtually ensure that you never run out of bags, leave a battery uncharged, or sit by the side of a lonely highway: the checklist. Checklists are simple and powerful tools, and most of us don't use them effectively or enough. In the press of fieldwork, it's all to easy too forget one or two simple things. A checklist lets you place your brain on cruise control to focus on those things for just as long as it take to run through the list. You don't have to worry about remembering things—the checklist remembers for you.

As with any kind of tool, building an effective checklist takes a bit of work. Review the equipment and supplies you're going to need in the field or lab and list everything: shovels, trowels, screens, transits, cameras—anything and everything you might need to do your proposed work. This comprehensive equipment list is what you'll use to build your checklist, so make sure anything you might need is listed.

The next step is to do the same thing with supplies, those things you're going to use up. Write down all of the supplies you can imagine needing, everything from pencils to protractors to toilet paper. You can estimate quantities if you want, but the critical thing is to get it all down on paper.

The last and most often ignored step is operations. Make a list of each thing that needs to be done every day before you go to the field and after you return. This includes tasks like loading the equipment into the trucks, making sure there is gas for the pump, and recharging the batteries for the TDS. Write down everything and anything you can think of and when it needs to be done.

In the planning stage, these lists can help in budgeting. In the field, take the complete list and edit it down to reflect the real-world needs. A lot of stuff you planned for may be superfluous, and you probably forgot some stuff. Combine your equipment, supplies, and chores lists on a single sheet of paper if at all possible. Print the lists on colored paper so you can find them easily. You might want to have separate setup and shutdown lists for each day. It's incredibly anal, but it works, and it will save you time and heartache.

Save your lists from each project. As you work on your proposal for the next one, you've got a good head start on the equipment and supplies you'll need for your new project.

Here are three sample lists from the Higgins project, a CRM project we conducted several years ago in central Texas.

Equipment Checklist

Equipment	Number Needed	On Hand?
Excavation Equipment		
Flat-bladed shovels	8	
Round shovels	8	
Entrenching tools	8	
Pick mattock	2	
Rake	1	
Wheelbarrows	6	
Plumb bobs	2	
Folding saws	4	
Pointed trowels	12	
Square trowels	12	
Line levels	12	
Knee pads	12	
Saw horses	10	
25-m tape measures	4	
100-m tape measures	1	
10-m tape measures	12	
Field scale	1	
5-pound hammer	1	
Claw hammer	1	
Hand saw	1	
Electric drill	1	
Nails/screws/staples	Box	
1/4-inch screens	6	
1/2-inch screens	2	
1/8-inch screens	2	
Folding tables (lab also)	6	
Folding chairs (lab also)	12	
5-gallon buckets (plastic)	12	
3-gallon buckets (metal)	12	
Dustpans	12	
Whisk brooms	12	
Corner pins	100	
Set out pins	25	
Survey/Mapping Equipment		
Optical (4 screw) transit	1	
Transit tripod	1	
Ranging pole	1	
Stadia rod	1	
TDS	1	
TDS tripod	1	
3-centimeter TDS targets	2	
1-centimeter TDS targets (peanuts)	2	

Continued

Equipment Checklist (*continued*)

Equipment	Number Needed	On Hand?
Extendable target poles	4	
50-centimeter target poles	2	
TDS quick charger	1	
TDS overnight charger	1	
TDS battery	2	
SDR-33 data collector	1	
SDR-33 field case	1	
SDR-33 serial cable	1	
SDR-33 Hirose to DB9 connector	1	
Brunton compass	1	
Datum markers	25	
TDS/SDR manuals	1	
Transit/TDS field book	1	

Computer Equipment

Laptop computers	3	
Desktop computer	1	
Dot matrix printer	2	
100-foot extension cords	1	
25-foot extension cords	3	
6-outlet surge suppressors	4	
Mice	4	
Mouse pads	4	
Printer cables	2	
DB9F-DB25F serial cables	2	
Null modem cable—DB9F-DB9M	2	
Modem	1	
Boot disk (DOS6.22)	4	

Field Lab/Field Office Equipment

Calipers	2	
Stapler	4	
Metal rulers	4	
3-hole punch	2	
Tape dispenser	2	
Lab scale	1	
3-hole 1.5-inch binders	12	
File boxes	3	
Hanging file folders	100	
Camera	4	
Camera tripod	2	
Camera case	4	
Photo log	2	
Pencil sharpener	2	
Hand lenses	2	
Labeling pens	6	

Supplies—verify inventory in field box daily

Pin flags	100
String	2 rolls
Burlap bags	20
Large paper bags	100
Small paper bags	100
Big Ziploc bags	100
Medium Ziploc bags	100
Small Ziploc bags	400
Pin fed 3 × 5 cards	200
Pin fed 8 1/2 × 11-inch computer paper	500 sheets
Printer ribbons	2
#2 pencils	48—2 boxes
Erasers	6
Stick pens—black	12
Sharpies—fine-point	20
Sharpies—medium-point	10
SDR33 batteries—9-volt	6
SDR33 batteries—backup	2
Staples	1 box
Flagging tape—red	6 rolls
Flagging tape—orange	6 rolls
Flagging tape—yellow	6 rolls
Aluminum foil	3 rolls
Toilet paper	6 rolls
Film—color	12 rolls
Film—B&W	12 rolls
File folders	50
Strat forms	100
Sample forms	100
Photo log pages	100

Daily Operations Checklist

Daily Loading
  (equipment not housed at
    the site in the field office)—Morning—at field house
Field office boxes
Artifact/sample boxes
Soil sample bags
Rock sample bags
Water screen buckets
  (5-gallon plastic)
Laptops
TDS
Extra TDS battery
SDR33
Cameras
Water
Vehicle fuel

Daily cleanup—At site—shut down
All flagged artifacts shot
  in with TDS
Field equipment in trailer
Tarp open units
Laptops to field house
Tables under trailer
Electrical power disconnected,
  cords in trailer
TDS broken down—to field
  house
Cameras to field house
Inventory field office supplies
Collected artifact numbers
  verified
Collected sample numbers
  verified
Artifacts and samples to field
  house

Daily Check-in—At field house/lab—daily
Check artifacts and samples in
  to field lab
Reconcile provenience
  problems, etc., from
  previous day's artifacts and
  samples
Download SDR33

Continued

Daily Operations Checklist (*continued*)

Daily Check-in—At field house/lab—daily (*continued*)

Create Daily.dat backup file
  on floppy
Delete SDR33 jobs
Verify status of SDR33 backup
  batteries (change if low)
Create updated strat list for lab
Create updated provenience
  list for lab
Vacuum field computers
Vacuum field printer
Update lab database from
  field computers
Back up lab computer
  database
Place TDS battery on charger
Install charged TDS battery
  on TDS

REFERENCES

Binford, Lewis R.
  1983 *In Pursuit of the Past*. Thames and Hudson, New York. Most
        approachable book from America's leading and most
        controversial archaeological thinker.

Black, Stephen L.
  1993 Nailing the Coffin Shut on the Traditional Approach to
        Prehistoric Archeology in Texas: An Epitaph and Inquiry into
        the Afterlife. *CRM News and Views* 5(1):16–19. Critique of
        archaeology by default as practiced mainly by CRM
        archaeologists.

Black, Stephen L., Kevin Jolly, Charles D. Frederick, Jason R. Lucas, James
W. Karbula, Paul R. Takac, and Daniel R. Potter
  1998 *Investigations and Experimentation at the Higgins Site
        (41BX184—Module 3)*, 2 volumes, Studies in Archeology 27.
        Texas Archeological Research Laboratory, University of Texas
        at Austin. An atypical CRM report in which Black and Jolly
        attempt to practice what they preach.

Blanton, Dennis B.
  1995 The Case for CRM Training in Academic Institutions. *SAA
        Bulletin* 13(4):40–41.

Butler, William B.
  1987 Significance and Other Frustrations in the CRM Process.
        American Antiquity 52(4):820–29.

Carnett, Carol
  1991 *Legal Background of Archeological Resources Protection*.
        Technical Brief No. 11. U.S. Department of the Interior,
        National Park Service. Technical speak by a lawyer.

Cheek, Annetta L.
   1991   Protection of Archaeological Resources on Public Lands:
          History of the Archaeological Resources Protection Act. In
          George S. Smith and John E. Ehrenhard, eds., *Protecting the
          Past*, CRC Press, Boca Raton, Florida. Reviews ARPA.

Ebert, James I.
   1992   *Distributional Archaeology*. University of New Mexico Press,
          Albuquerque. Theoretical take on the landscape approach.

Flannery, Kent V., ed.
   1976   *The Early Mesoamerican Village*. Academic Press, New York.
          Classic study useful for its discussion of sampling strategies.

Friedman, Janet L.
   1996   The Business of Archaeology: Planning the Work of Cultural
          Resource Compliance. *SAA Bulletin* 14(5):22–24.

Green, Ernestene L., ed.
   1984   *Ethics and Values in Archaeology*. Free Press, New York.
          Edited volume with useful discussions of ethics in CRM
          archaeology.

Green, William, and John F. Doershuk
   1998   Cultural Resource Management and American Archaeology.
          Journal of Archaeological Research 6(2):121–67. Useful review
          of subject and literature.

Jameson, John H. Jr., John E. Ehrenhard, and Wilfred M. Husted
   1990   *Federal Archeological Contracting: Utilizing the Competitive
          Procurement Process*. Archeological Assistance Program,
          Technical Brief 7. Bureaucratic process.

Johnson, Ronald W., and Michael G. Schene
   1987   *Cultural Resource Management*. Robert E. Krieger Publishing,
          Malabar, Florida.

Kerber, Jordan E., ed.
   1994   *Cultural Resource Management: Archaeological Research,
          Preservation Planning, and Public Education in the
          Northeastern United States*. Bergin and Garvey, Westport,
          Connecticut. Useful examples of how CRM has affected the
          archaeology of one region.

King, Thomas F.
   1998   *Cultural Resource Laws and Practice: An Introductory Guide*.
          AltaMira Press, Walnut Creek, California. Must-read for any
          budding CRM archaeologist, written by the principal architect
          of federal CRM laws.

2000 *Federal Planning and Historic Places: The Section 106 Process.* AltaMira Press, Walnut Creek, California. Another practical guidebook to CRM.

Lyon, Edwin A.
1996 *A New Deal for Southeastern Archaeology.* University of Alabama Press, Tuscaloosa. History of early years of government funded archaeology.

McGimsey, Charles R. III
1985 This, Too, Will Pass: Moss-Bennett in Perspective. *American Antiquity* 50(2):326–31. Historical perspective on AHPA and NHPA.
1998 Headwaters: How the Postwar Boom Boosted Archeology. *Common Ground* 3(2/3):16–21. Historical essay on formative years of federally funded archaeology.

Mueller, James W., ed.
1979 *Sampling in Archaeology.* University of Arizona Press, Tucson. Useful edited volume reflecting emphasis on the subject in 1960s and 1970s.

Neumann, Loretta
1991 The Politics of Archaeology and Historical Preservation: How Our Laws Are Really Made. In George S. Smith and John E. Ehrenhard, eds., *Protecting the Past*, pp. 41–46. CRC Press, Boca Raton, Florida. Title says it all; author was the SAA's lobbyist.

Preucel, Robert W., ed.
1991 *Processual and Postprocessual Archaeologists: Multiple Ways of Knowing the Past.* Occasional Paper 10, Center for Archaeological Investigations, Southern Illinois University at Carbondale. Papers from archaeologists of many different theoretical perspectives, some of them—papers and perspectives—quite dense.

Raab, L. Mark, Timothy C. Klinger, Michael B. Schiffer, and Albert C. Goodyear
1980 Clients, Contracts, and Profits: Conflicts in Public Archaeology. *American Anthropologist* 82(3):539–55. Early discussion of tension created by archaeology as a private business.

Renfrew, Colin, and Paul Bahn
2000 *Archaeology: Theories, Methods, and Practice.* 3d edition. Thames and Hudson, New York. Introductory textbook from a British perspective with useful explanations of contrasting theoretical approaches.

Rossignol, Jacqueline, and LuAnn Wandsnider, eds.
1992   *Space, Time, and Archaeological Landscapes.* Plenum Press,
       New York. Method and theory of landscape approaches.

Schuldenrein, Joseph
1995   The Care and Feeding of Archaeologists: A Plea for
       Pragmatic Training in the 21st Century. *SAA Bulletin*
       13(3):22–24.
1998   The Changing Career Paths and the Training of Professional
       Archaeologists: Observations from the Barnard College
       Forum—Part I. *SAA Bulletin* 16(1):31–33.
1999   The Changing Career Paths and the Training of Professional
       Archaeologists: Observations from the Barnard College
       Forum—Part II. *SAA Bulletin* 17(1):26–29.

Simpson, Kay
1999   Business 101: The Mysteries of Billable Hours, Overhead, and
       Contracts. *ACRA Edition* 5(6):1–5. Excellent overview of how
       the costs of CRM projects are calculated and billed from a
       business perspective.

Snyder, David
1995   Cinderella's Choice: The Emerging Role of the State Historic
       Preservation Office in Cultural Resource Management. *SAA
       Bulletin* 13(5):19–21. SHPO 101.

Thomas, David Hurst
1997   *Archaeology.* 3d ed, Harcourt Brace College, Fort Worth, Texas.
       Approachable introductory textbook from an American
       perspective with good examples of basic concepts.

Wandsnider, LuAnn
1996   Describing and Comparing Archaeological Spatial Structures.
       Journal of Archaeological Method and Theory 3(4):319–84.
       Useful theoretical and methodological discussion of site
       structure.

Waters, Michael R.
1992   *Principles of Geoarchaeology: A North American Perspective.*
       University of Arizona Press, Tucson. Good introductory text
       on subject.

Watson, Patty Jo, Steven A. LeBlanc, and Charles L. Redman
1984   *Archaeological Explanation: The Scientific Method in
       Archaeology.* Columbia University Press, New York.
       Theoretical primer from a processualist perspective.

Welch, James M.
  1993   From Archaeological Field Crew to Business Administration.
          Practicing Anthropology 15(1):9–11. Personal view of a CRM
          career and training.

Willey, Gordon R., and Jeremy A. Sabloff
  1993   *A History of American Archaeology.* 3d ed. W. H. Freeman,
          New York. Latest edition of this standard reference includes
          some discussion of the impact of CRM on American
          archaeology.

Zeder, Melinda A.
  1997   *The American Archaeologist—A Profile.* AltaMira Press,
          Walnut Creek, California. Results of survey of SAA members.

 # INDEX

Note: Throughout the index, *CRM* is used in place of *cultural resource management*.

ABOUT THE AUTHORS AND SERIES EDITORS

Stephen L. Black is a research associate and editor of www. TexasBeyondHistory.net at the Texas Archeological Research Laboratory at the University of Texas at Austin. He has been involved with CRM archaeology since 1975 and has done shovel testing, project administration, and almost everything in between. Steve has a Ph.D. from Harvard, an M.A. from the University of Texas at San Antonio, and a B.A. from the University of Texas at Austin, all focusing on anthropological archaeology. Most of his CRM research has centered on hunter-gatherer archaeology. Steve has been fortunate enough to be able to design and carry out mitigation projects at four significant hunter-gatherer sites in south and central Texas. He has also directed the analysis and reporting of five excavation projects that were begun by others. Through such experiences, he has developed an attitude about accomplishing meaningful research in the real world of archaeology. Steve's other research interests include experimental archaeology, hot rock technology, field methodology, information technology, and public archaeology. When not doing archaeology, he enjoys sailing, fishing, traveling, writing, experimenting with fermentation science, and having fun without his clothes on.

Kevin Jolly is a research fellow of the Texas Archeological Research Laboratory at the University of Texas at Austin and the vice president of technology at RW3 Technologies, Inc. In the late 1970s and early 1980s, he was a contract archaeologist working in Texas, New Mexico, and the southeastern United States. Starting in 1993, along with Steve Black and Dan Potter, Kevin helped put together a series of innovative (controversial) archaeological projects including the Higgins Experiment. To support the data collection efforts of these projects,

Kevin designed and built an archaeological data management system integrating total data stations and field computers. In the late 1990s, he directed the Historical Sites Atlas Project for the Texas Historical Commission, developing a comprehensive GIS database of Texas archaeological and historic sites. His research interests are archaeological data design, data collection, and data management.

Larry J. Zimmerman is the head of the Archaeology Department of the Minnesota Historical Society. He served as an adjunct professor of anthropology and visiting professor of American Indian and Native Studies at the University of Iowa from 1996 to 2002 and as chair of the American Indian and Native Studies Program from 1998 to 2001. He earned his Ph.D. in anthropology at the University of Kansas in 1976. Teaching at the University of South Dakota for twenty-two years, he left there in 1996 as Distinguished Regents Professor of Anthropology.

While in South Dakota, he developed a major CRM program and the University of South Dakota Archaeology Laboratory, where he is still a research associate. He was named the University of South Dakota Student Association Teacher of the Year in 1980, given the Burlington Northern Foundation Faculty Achievement Award for Outstanding Teaching in 1986, and granted the Burlington Northern Faculty Achievement Award for Research in 1990. He was selected by Sigma Xi, the Scientific Research Society, as a national lecturer from 1991 to 1993, and he served as executive secretary of the World Archaeological Congress from 1990 to 1994. He has published more than three hundred articles, CRM reports, and reviews and is the author, editor, or coeditor of fifteen books, including *Native North America* (with Brian Molyneaux, University of Oklahoma Press, 2000) and *Indians and Anthropologists: Vine Deloria, Jr., and the Critique of Anthropology* (with Tom Biolsi, University of Arizona Press, 1997). He has served as the editor of *Plains Anthropologist* and the *World Archaeological Bulletin* and as the associate editor of *American Antiquity*. He has done archaeology in the Great Plains of the United States and in Mexico, England, Venezuela, and Australia. He has also worked closely with a wide range of American Indian nations and groups.

William Green is Director of the Logan Museum of Anthropology and Adjunct Professor of Anthropology at Beloit College, Beloit, Wisconsin. He has been active in archaeology since 1970. Having grown up on the

south side of Chicago, he attributes his interest in archaeology and anthropology to the allure of the exotic (i.e., rural) and a driving urge to
learn the unwritten past, abetted by the opportunities available at the
city's museums and universities. His first field work was on the Mis-
sissippi River bluffs in western Illinois. Although he also worked in Is-
rael and England, he returned to Illinois for several years of survey and
excavation. His interests in settlement patterns, ceramics, and archaeobotany developed there. He received his Master's degree from the
University of Wisconsin–Madison and then served as Wisconsin SHPO
staff archaeologist for eight years. After obtaining his Ph.D. from
UW–Madison in 1987, he served as State Archaeologist of Iowa from
1988 to 2001, directing statewide research and service programs including burial site protection, geographic information, publications,
contract services, public outreach, and curation. His main research interests focus on the development and spread of native agriculture. He
has served as editor of the *Midcontinental Journal of Archaeology* and
The Wisconsin Archeologist, has published articles in *American Antiquity, Journal of Archaeological Research,* and other journals, and has
received grants and contracts from the National Science Foundation,
National Park Service, Iowa Humanities Board, and many other agencies and organizations.